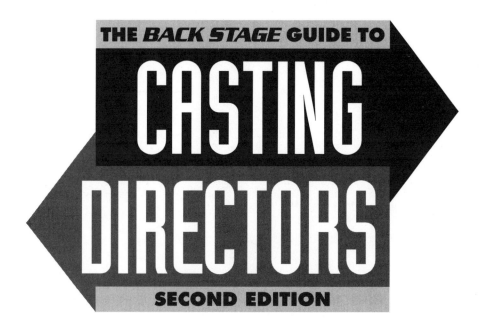

THE *BACK STAGE* GUIDE TO
CASTING DIRECTORS
SECOND EDITION

HETTIE LYNNE HURTES

BACK STAGE BOOKS
an imprint of Watson-Guptill Publications/New York

Published in 1998 in the United States
by Back Stage Books, an imprint of Watson-Guptill Publications,
a division of BPI Communications, Inc.,
1515 Broadway, New York, NY 10036-8986.

Library of Congress Cataloging-in-Publication Data for this title can be
obtained by writing to the Library of Congress, Washington, D.C. 20540

Manufactured in the United States of America

ISBN 0-8230-8806-5

Editor: Dale Ramsey
Designer: Bob Fillie, Graphiti Graphics
Production manager: Hector Campbell

1 2 3 4 5 / 02 01 00 99 98

To my Dad

Contents

PART ONE:
THE CASTING DIRECTORS

PART TWO:
THE CASTING PROCESS

PART THREE:
WHERE TO FIND CASTING DIRECTORS

Acknowledgments

I express my gratitude to Back Stage Books and their editor, Dale Ramsey, for their commitment to *The Back Stage Guide to Casting Directors*. Five years ago, the publisher recognized the need for a compilation of profiles of top casting directors across the country, and because of the strong response from aspiring actors and others in show business the publisher realized the need to update the guide periodically. Thus this second edition.

I also thank my assistants who did the necessary transcribing of my many interviews through the months preceding publication. They include Myrna Kranz, Robyn Latter, and Barbara Adams.

Thanks, too, to the Casting Society of America and to Breakdown Services for their meticulous updating of casting director information, without which it would have been virtually impossible to compile this edition. Casting directors are notorious for their nomadic lifestyle, and both CSA and Breakdown provided an invaluable service.

To all the casting directors who took their much valued time away from their duties to grant me interviews, I heartily express my gratitude, and I hope that through their comments and insights the actors who pass through their portals will be better prepared for that coveted audition.

And, of course, my gratitude to my family: my husband, Ron, our two daughters, Jennifer and Aubrey, and my son, Brandon, for allowing me the many hours at my word processor to churn out this all-consuming project. You guys are the best!

Thank you, one and all.

H.L.H.
Los Angeles, March 1998

Introduction

If you're looking for a book full of juicy Hollywood or Broadway gossip, and you're hoping to read all about the alleged "casting couch," sorry to disappoint you—you've selected the wrong title. This book has a lot of inside information, but not the sort suitable for the tabloids. Instead, what you'll glean here is tailored to those within the profession who are hungry for more background on a little known area of the industry, casting, and those who comprise the field, casting directors.

In Hollywood, prior to the onset of television, during the heyday of the studio system, the motion-picture studio selected the stars, carefully groomed them, and placed them before the cameras to determine their ultimate fate. The golden era of the studio system began its decline in the 1950s, but even as late as the 1960s an established casting profession didn't exist.

"It was like ordering a Chinese meal: one from column A and one from Column B," explains Marion Dougherty, senior vice president of feature film casting for Warner Brothers, recalling her early days in the business. The studios, she remembers, would simply recycle from their ranks. "That's why you'd always see the same actor cast in the same kind of role—cliché casting." Dougherty was a pioneer: She was the first casting director to set up her own office, in 1965, on Manhattan's East Side, where apparently no one in show business had previously set foot.

She started casting in the late '40s, while employed by the advertising agency that was producing the acclaimed Kraft Television Theater. "No one knew what we were doing. I did what seemed to work for me, which was calling people in and reading them for something, and then whittling it down to a couple of people I thought were right, and then bringing them in to read for the director." Marion found these actors on Broadway, where, at the same time Shirley Rich, another casting director, was helping Rodgers and Hammerstein increase their roster of actors. Most producers and directors in those days did their own casting, Rich recalls, but Rodgers and Hammerstein, along with the imperious Broadway producer David Merrick and a few others, hired someone else to undertake the task. "I always had an open-door policy," she explains. "I met all the actors, went to all the auditions, and kept extensive files."

It wasn't until Rich was hired by MGM as a talent scout that she became involved in film, and even then she didn't cast specific projects but found talent the studio might be interested in placing under contract for future films. In 1969, she opened her own office in New York and was able to cast for individual producers.

When Marion Dougherty was hiring actors for television projects in New York, most had only stage experience. In the early '60s, Dougherty was asked to cast *The Naked City*, a dramatic series. "It became the New York actor's screening place for Hollywood," she recollects fondly. "The studios would see these new faces and would immediately bring them to Hollywood." These faces belonged to actors such as Alan Alda and Dustin Hoffman.

Dougherty began to establish an impressive reputation in her fledgling field. She was hired in 1964 to cast a feature film for director George Roy Hill, the first major motion picture to be shot in New York since the days of D.W. Griffith's Biograph studios. Titled *The World of Henry Orient*, the movie marked Peter Sellers' American film debut.

The following year, Dougherty was brought to Los Angeles to cast *Hawaii*, not an easy task. Since there was no established casting system, no filing cabinets of pictures and résumés, Dougherty had an uphill battle trying to find Polynesian actors. She turned to MGM, which had hired Polynesian cast members for the remake (with Marlon Brando) of *Mutiny on the Bounty*. Unfortunately, they hadn't kept files on the film. Dougherty had to start from scratch.

A decade later, in 1976, Dougherty set up a casting office in Los Angeles. She didn't know it at the time, but she had cast the die, so to speak. Her rudimentary system has since evolved into a sophisticated, highly competitive, and lucrative business. The only other casting director on the West Coast at the time was Lynn Stalmaster (now retired after a much celebrated career representing clients such as Sidney Pollack and Brian DePalma).

Today, casting directors are among the first creative forces to be brought aboard a project, and their names are prominently featured in the opening credits—a definitive indication, in Hollywood at least, of the value of these professionals. Some are put on staff by major studios and television networks, but most are in business as independents to be hired either by a production company or by the producer of a particular film, television show, or stage production.

Before a deal is "inked," the casting director is sent a script. Once he or she has read the material, the next step is a series of sometimes arduous sessions with the producer and director to discuss the essentials and the nuances of each character in the script. The casting director will offer suggestions as to who might fit the bill. Most casting directors readily admit that casting must be a collaborative effort. "You develop a certain communication in terms of understanding a director's approach," observes Stalmaster.

David Rubin, a former Stalmaster protégé, regards the initial exploration of the characters as one of the most critical periods in the movie casting process. But, he adds, casting is a process of "continual discussion and re-exploration. It's vitally important," he observes, "to take all the existing elements into consideration."

Having examined the elements of each character with the producer and casting director, the director tells the latter which actors he or she would prefer to read. This brings us to the question of who really casts a project. There is no definitive answer. It depends on the project and on the director. Certainly the actors for the leading roles are, for the most part, selected by the director or producer, or, in the case of a major TV production, the network itself. The supporting cast, however, is usually the bailiwick of the casting director. Still, there are times when a casting director has a great deal of influence on the selection of an actor for a major role. Take the movie *Night Shift,* for example. Jane Jenkins explains that Brian Grazer and Ron Howard were intent on John Belushi for the lead, but after auditioning Michael Keaton for another project the three were working on, she was determined to give him a shot at *Night Shift.* "So when Ron and Brian were still contemplating Belushi," recalls Jenkins, "I did half an hour on why I thought it would be much more exciting to hire Keaton and discover somebody new." Her persistence paid off: Keaton won the role.

Like the first edition of *The Back Stage Guide to Casting Directors,* this fully rewritten second edition explores the various methods used by fifty-eight of the entertainment industry's prominent casting directors when filling the roles in stage, film, or television projects. It does this through profile/interviews with people in the field who describe the different techniques employed to cast particular projects and explain what qualities and acting experience they look for in the actors they consider.

In the following pages are related many candid observsations on how these professionals view the craft of acting; how actors can prepare for and be effective in auditions, how they should conduct themselves during an interview, and, generally, what actors can expect when they're being considered for a part. Accompanying each profile is a sample list of that casting director's credits and the address to which actors may submit material.

Most producers and directors enthusiastically endorse the importance of casting directors in the creation of any contemporary production. Producer-director Frank Marshall, whose solo credits include *Arachnophobia* and *Milk Money*, began his career as part of Steven Spielberg's team. He states that "the casting director works with all the agents—I would never have enough time." But casting directors bring much more to a project than administrative support. Academy Award–winning director Robert Wise plays homage to the casting director's creative prowess: "Their biggest contribution to most pictures is the supporting cast. They bring you the whole range." And actor-director Sondra Locke gives the casting director credit for providing the director with the best talent available. "I've always said you can take the exact same film and make it the exact same way with six different sets of actors, and you'll have six different films. It's just that critical what an individual actor brings to the screen and to the role."

In *The Back Stage Guide to Casting Directors*, I have attempted to shed light on a profession that other authors who advise the actor have left largely unexamined. Not just actors, but also directors, producers, agents, and other artists in the entertainment business will savor these casting directors' insights into a fascinating and important part of the creative process. Actors wanting to eliminate some of those gnawing anxieties all too prevalent in the continual business of landing a job should find these casting directors especially illuminating. Indeed, any reader interested in the entertainment business may be assured of finding this book an eye-opening, behind-the-scenes glimpse into the creation of this country's best motion pictures, television shows, and theater productions.

PART ONE

The Casting Directors

Julie Alter

c/o Casting Society of America
606 N. Larchmont Blvd. #4B
Los Angeles, CA 90004
(213) 463-1925
FAX (213) 463-5753

Julie Alter is a nomad, as are many casting directors in Los Angeles. She's changed locations so often, it isn't even an issue. She has moved from in-house casting director for the Manhattan Theatre Club, to the offices of *thirtysomething*, in partnership with Susan Young, to a solo suite in West Hollywood, and then on to a tiny office in a nondescript industrial section of North Hollywood, where she cast a series of short films for Showtime.

Tucked away in her office, the brick walls bedecked with her youngster's "masterpieces," Alter is the proverbial busy bee. When she is not on the phone, she reads actors for *Rebel Highway*, the series of remakes of those now-camp 1950s teen-angst movies.

"I try to make the breakdowns as open as possible," she explained, and she'll bring in a variety of types for each role unless a producer has been quite specific. "The most frustrating thing about my job," Alter admits, "is when you think someone's really right for a role, and the director or producer doesn't see it that way. They just don't see the talent. They judge them differently."

Alter feels that her theatrical training in New York is responsible for her empathy. "I understand where actors are coming from, and I'm able to help them through the audition process. I can empathize with them and provide them with a sense of what the director wants from them." Alter provides a great deal of information to actors at auditions. She spends a lot of time redirecting them and giving adjustments, acting almost as a coach.

"I love actors," she says, "but I don't love what the sys-

CREDITS INCLUDE:
L.A. Firefighters Pilot
Rebel Highway
The Red Coat
The Last Temptation of Christ
thirtysomething
Teddy Roosevelt & the Rough Riders
Location casting

tem does to them out here. I like them in their purest form. In New York, it's more provincial. There's more communication and support between the casting community and actors. Out here, there are hundreds of us and thousands of day players paying SAG insurance. The stakes are higher, and there's more desperation in trying to make a living, which turns casting directors off, in general. But when it gets down to the essential acting community, and those who are in it for the right reasons, I don't think it becomes a we/they situation."

The most important element of an actor's craft, to Alter, is his or her inner voice. "It's that critical eye during the audition. The more work actors have done, the emotional preparation for a role, the more focused they can be on the material, rather than letting the critic come into their head, which always screws them up." In other words, Alter believes that actors must stay focused on the material and on the work they're doing at the time. "The less importance actors place on each audition, the better they're going to be," she adds. "Therefore, the more auditions they go out on, the better, so that each experience becomes less important."

She compares an audition to a job interview. "If a person has only one interview that month, he or she is going to fret over what to wear rather than concentrate on the job. It's the same thing with actors.

"If an actor has a devil-may-care attitude, I'll want to look further. That actor makes me go to him or her, rather than coming here to please me; there are twenty-five people a day who do that."

Alter appreciates an actor who's well trained, but because she isn't as familiar with schools and teachers out here as she was in New York, it's not as critical. "I try to be a lot more democratic," she explains. "Some people know their natural talent, and if they're right for a role, then studying doesn't come into play as much." What Alter is looking for is a combination of experience and training. A résumé complete with film and regional and professional theater will catch her eye, but it's who these individuals are as actors when they come in to read that is most important.

Alter finds her actors through theater, on cable television, and from submissions, among other venues. "I look at all the photos that come across my desk. I try to at least glance at everything." She's not concerned whether an actor has an agent if he or she is right for the role. "I'm less judgmental than I used to be. It's happened that I've passed on people, and a year later I'll see them and realize they had a special talent that I missed. It's the same as when you see a dress on the rack, but because it was the wrong color for the occasion, you wouldn't even consider it."

Professional showcases are another venue Alter frequents in her eternal talent search. "I'll never go to paid showcases—never. It's a hideous cottage industry. I feel very strongly about that. I don't want anyone to have to pay to see me."

She recommends that any actor considering a class audit it first and network with other actors to find good teachers.

Regarding dos and don'ts in a casting session, Alter, a former actress herself, is extremely liberal. "Actors can do anything they want to do," she insists. "Actors usually put their problems aside when they come in for an audition. They're usually nice to me when I'm having a bad day. They're on their best behavior, but I wouldn't tell an actor what to do or what not to do. It's all in their work."

Dress is also unimportant to Alter, and she suggests an actor put as little effort as possible into impressing her. "It's nice if you wash your hair, but I don't have guidelines. It's our job to see the actor through the wrong clothes, through the dirty hair. We have to be flexible."

She's also not easily embarrassed. She once had to find actors with cute rear ends for *Dream On*, a risqué series which ran for several years on HBO. "So instead of asking the ladies to take their tops off, which we've had to do, I had to ask the guys to come in and moon for us. At least they got to see what women have to go through!" It didn't even faze her when one actress kissed her on the mouth. "True, I'll never forget it, but that was what she felt she had to do. An actor can do whatever he wants, short of getting me pregnant!"

Alter's most satisfying moments come when she finds the actors who are really right for the job. "Almost every kid in every one of these *Rebel Highway* segments has unique qualities, like David Arquette. It's very exciting, because they're only about nineteen, and I get to 'discover' them and help them move forward with their careers."

Julie Alter is very supportive of talent, and encourages actors to keep going out even when they don't get the roles. She does suggest, however, that if, after five years or so, they're still trying to make ends meet, they should consider another field. "Just don't be discouraged by negative feedback from casting directors," she advises. "They're just opinions."

Deborah Aquila

PARAMOUNT PICTURES

Associates: Sarah Finn, Dayna Polehanki
5555 Melrose Ave.
Bob Hope Bldg. #206
Los Angeles, CA 90038
(213) 956-5444
FAX (213) 862-1371

Deborah Aquila, Senior Vice President of Feature Casting at Paramount Pictures, is a trained actress, having studied for four years with the celebrated Stella Adler, in New York. To Aquila, training is essential: "It's as important to me as a residency is to a medical student." When she decided to make the transition to casting, her belief in proper training led her to work with Bonnie Timmerman, whom she calls "the Godmother of Casting." Says Aquila of her mentor, "She's a wonderful woman, and I learned from her how to go for the interesting and not the obvious. I learned how to cast just right and left of center, never to hit it right on the nose. I also learned from her how to be persistent in searching for the right actor for the role—basically, never to stop when you think you have something, but rather to stop when you *know* you have it."

Casting is a process, Aquila explains. "Over the course of reading the same sides week after week, the characters start to evolve in the director's mind, and roles begin to become clearer with each session. It's important for the actor to have a clear point of view of the character, with strong choices, before the audition."

The persistence Aquila learned from her mentor was far and away most evident in her casting of *Primal Fear*. Aquila saw no less than two thousand actors for the role eventually captured by Edward Norton. "It was a very hard role to cast," she observes. "It had to be done truthfully on three different levels, and each transition had to be completely believable. There's no way an actor could fudge this role." For nearly

CREDITS INCLUDE:
Mother
Primal Fear
The Shawshank Redemption
sex, lies and videotape
Last Exit to Brooklyn

six months, Aquila and her two associates scoured the world for talent. "We would see, on average, sixty actors a day, compare notes at the end of the day, put those we liked on tape, and present the tape to the director. Only two or three actors really stood out, but then, on the last leg of our search, in New York, Edward Norton walked through the door—and as far as I was concerned, the search was over." That's what Aquila refers to as star quality, later validated by others in the business. "Within three weeks, right after his two screen tests for *Primal Fear,* he was cast in Woody Allen's *Everybody Says I Love You,* and *The People vs. Larry Flynt.*"

She can't totally define "star quality," but Aquila believes it's a certain confidence which empowers the actor to embrace a character fully and completely with no inhibition. "Spontaneity and creativity happens," she adds, "when an actor is completely confident in his or her ability, which some acting studios term the relaxed actor. I call it the confident actor."

Aquila believes that training doesn't stop with school. She feels the best way to continue to study the craft is to do as much theater as possible. All the actors she cast in *Last Exit to Brooklyn* came out of the theater. Laura San Giacomo had been admired for her work in a play called *Beirut* when she was brought in to read for *sex, lies, and videotape.* Michael Rappaport's first feature was *Zebrahead; Last Exit to Brooklyn* was Sam Rockwell's and Alexis Arquette's first feature film; and *Primal Fear* was the big stepping-stone for Edward Norton.

Aquila expects every actor at an audition to be completely prepared. "It's very important to the process. If I'm prepared and have done my homework, I expect the same from any actor who walks through the door." She expects the actor to understand the material fully. "I think it's important the actors create a situation in their mind's eye, so that when they come in, they have a total sense of what the script and character are." She also feels it imperative that actors read the entire script, whether for a feature or a pilot, so they can create a proper background for their characters. While she doesn't expect them to know their lines by heart, it's important to Aquila that they be familiar with the material so they don't have their nose buried in the sides during the audition. She'll also talk to actors before an audition to help them relax and find out what is their "take" on the character in general. "If the backstory needs to be adjusted slightly, we'll discuss the finer points of the characterization in greater detail so that the actor can understand what the director needs in the role." She may also try to get a feel for what actors understand about the characters by asking where they come from and what they do for a living, and about the relationship between certain characters and the basic objectives. "Then, if the answers are just a bit off, I'll adjust them and share with them what the director has in mind."

Aquila doesn't always follow the script to the letter. She enjoys trying to cast against type. The casting of Jennifer Jason Leigh is a good example. "Jennifer had never done a role like TraLaLa in *Last Exit* in her film career to date. There wasn't any film or tape I could show the directors and producers that was relevant to this character. Therefore, the physical transformation had to happen in the room, which she succeeded in doing. Here was a case where the character of TraLaLa was headed in a very different direction in our minds. When Jennifer showed us her version, she got the role."

Seeing a lot of stage actors, Aquila knows that some can easily make the transition to film, others cannot. "It's sometimes difficult for an actor with years of experience on the stage to adjust to the level that TV and film require. More often than not the theater requires a broader interpretation. For the camera the levels of performance have to be adjusted to fit the medium." She believes a film director can help an actor through that process, and a casting director can aid in the transition as well.

If an actor wants to schedule an interview with Deborah Aquila, she asks that he or she send in a picture or résumé, and when she's not involved with a film, she'll try to set up either a meeting or a reading. So get that two-and-a-half-minute monologue polished and ready to go!

Lisa Beach

LISA BEACH CASTING

Associate: Sarah Katzman
c/o Casting Society of America
606 N. Larchmont Blvd. #4B
Los Angeles, CA 90004
(213) 463-1925

When you enter Lisa Beach's office, you'll find quite a few visual objects to help break the ice. You'll notice Beach's globetrotting photos, including a massive Mahi Mahi she caught off the coast of Hawaii. "If that can't draw somebody out," Beach exclaims, "I defy anyone else to do so!"

And draw them out she does, with her vivacious, youthful personality, which is probably responsible in part for her designation as "the casting expert on young people." Beach has cast such teen films as *School Ties, Calendar Girl, Scream,* and *Election,* for MTV Films.

Beach recently went from being vice president of casting for HBO to an independent casting director. At HBO, Beach supervised the casting process, hiring a casting director for each project the cable network planned to air. Now, she's back to on-line casting and the standard procedure: "Once I get the script, I'll read it and do a breakdown, listing all the characters, what page they appear on, and an appropriate budget for each role." She'll then audition the actors, have them read for the producers and director, and finally put them on tape.

One of her favorite steps in the process, she says, is reading with the actors. "I love it. I wouldn't have it any other way." And she really works with actors. "Here comes Scott now," she says with genuine anticipation. "Scott is here for the fourth time. I really want him to get this role." Scott is reading for a juicy part in *Election.* "When he came in the first time, he really hadn't gotten the essence of the character. He wasn't playing dumb enough. The role calls for a certain oafishness." The second time Scott came in, Beach admits, she was having a pretty

Credits include:
Election
Scream Parts 1 & 2
Citizen Ruth
Perversions of Science
Bad Influence

bad day and didn't want to have it affect the actor's performance. At a third session, Scott was beeped by his agent informing him of a network callback. "Now we can go over the scene, and I'll do it with him a hundred times if we need to. I just want him to nail it!"

Beach feels she has that special knack for spotting talent. She recalls her first casting breakthrough, as she calls it, when she was getting started in the business under the tutelage of David Rubin: "I was working on the *Dirty Dancing* television series when an actor named Tony Maggio came in. It was my first hands-on experience in casting, and I'd been reading many actors, thinking, 'Yeah, he's OK, he's OK.' But when Tony walked in and gave his reading, my eyes lit up and I said, 'Tony, can you just hold it? Stay right there. Don't move.' I ran into David's office and said, 'David, I think I'm having a breakthrough! I think I know what it is to be a great actor.' I told him who was in my office, and he simply said, 'Oh, yes, he's a wonderful actor. I think you're going to be all right.' I ultimately cast Tony in the movie *Bad Influence*."

There are actors who simply blow Beach away with their talent, and then there are those who blow themselves right out the door. For instance, there's the case of the actress who went a little too far. "I was casting a movie, and this particular woman came in to read the part of a seductive temptress," she recalls. "I knew she wasn't right when, at the beginning of the audition, in front of the producer and director, she came over to my chair and literally started fondling my hair and shoulders. If the part calls for shaking hands, fine, but please, don't ever kiss the casting director. I have taken a permanent moratorium on that actress. I'll never see her again."

Headshots that impress Beach are the ones she can stay with for more than two seconds, which is the average length of time she spends on a nondescript photo that comes across her desk. "There are so many that are interesting, creative, and soulful that the ones that aren't will just get sent to recycling." And while representation is important, Beach will consider an actor who's just getting started. "I've never actually cast someone from an unsolicited photo," she admits, "but I remember when I was doing *Scream*, there was this young man who wrote me a nice letter, and he had an interesting look. I called him in, and he wasn't bad. The role, unfortunately, was just too big for him to handle, but he definitely had something, and I encouraged him to keep going. Perseverance does pay."

Credits on the résumé are helpful, but every actor who walks into Beach's office need not have a wealth of experience. "Sometimes actors will have no credits at all, but if William Morris is willing to take a chance on them—even if they've only done one small feature at Sundance—that's fine with me. I'm more than happy to meet with an actor whom an agent of that caliber has faith in."

On *Scream*, two of the co-stars, Jamie Kennedy and Matthew Lillard, hadn't had much experience. "Even though Miramax wasn't as convinced as we were that Kennedy was right for the part, we were and wouldn't take no for an answer. He was born to play this character."

Beach doesn't do showcases, nor does she put much faith in them, for the most part. "I don't find them satisfying. The ones that offer to pay the casting director really appall me. I take a strong stand that actors shouldn't have to spend their hard-earned money to pay me to come to see them. That betokens a certain unprofessionalism on the part of the person organizing the showcase," she remarks. She admits that there are exceptions and that she does know some reputable actors who organize showcases she could vouch for. Still, she prefers the movies and theater for discovering new talent.

Whatever the actor decides to do to further his or her career, Beach believes it must be a concerted effort. "My best friend is an actress," she remarks. "Every single audition or part she's heard about or read for, every single bit of information she gets from her agents or other actors, she makes note of. If she hears or reads that a casting director has just had a baby, she'll jot it down, and if she happens to read for that person a year later, she'll make sure she asks, 'How's little Janie?'" Her friend has a successful TV career now. "I've seen what it took her to get there," says Beach with sincere admiration in her voice.

Breanna Benjamin

BREANNA BENJAMIN CASTING

406 W. 31st St., 15th floor
New York, NY 10001
(212) 279-9876

Breanna Benjamin is one of the more accessible casting directors in New York. She accepts photos and résumés from actors, whether or not they are represented by agents or are union members. For auditions, she realizes actors have to start somewhere, and if their type is right for the role she'll try to give them the opportunity to audition.

Benjamin, in fact, discovered the leading man in *True Love* from a picture he had submitted. "Neither the director nor producer thought he was right, but I convinced them to see him a second time and talk to him about changing his appearance just a bit, and to rethink his take on the character. Ron Eldard was cast in the lead; he has since signed with a prestige agent, starred in a TV series, starred on Broadway, and had several starring feature film roles."

Benjamin believes one of the most important attributes for actors is a "positive attitude about themselves. I find that the ones who make it most of the time like themselves and like the people around them. They like the world they live in. They're involved in the world they live in." Actors walk through her door everyday, but sometimes she can't get past their attitude to find out if they can act.

If Benjamin sees someone with potential she'll gladly pass along any advice the actor might seek. "I explain that, in many ways, acting is the same as working at IBM. It's a job. It's a career, but if it's the only thing in your life, you're not going to make it. You've heard of a banker or accountant mentality, and you know how boring that is.

"What makes you interesting is being a well-rounded person. That gives you the ability to make those flat words on the printed page into a well-rounded character"—it's the source of your talent.

At an interview, Benjamin expects to get to

CREDITS INCLUDE:
True Love
Joker's Wild
Outpost
All That Glitters
Survivor

know the actor as a person, but at the audition, she wants to see the character. "I want to see the change that takes place. There's nothing more frightening than an actor auditioning for a street hoodlum who comes in for an interview with that persona. It's scary. And this," she admits, "happens more times than you know." When an actor shows her only "the hoodlum," she isn't sure if this is his real demeanor or not—and if it is, she questions whether he also has the technique to sustain a performance.

Benjamin offers another pointer for actors interviewing with a casting director: Be prepared for the most common questions, such as, "Why don't you tell me about yourself?" "If they're smart, they should know that question will be asked, and it's just like learning a role. They should keep a one-minute set of notes in their diary on what they're going to talk about, so they don't just sit there and stutter and stammer." She suggests they keep updating those notes, especially if they've added something new to their lives.

A positive attitude should also be apparent at the audition. "In New York alone, there are thousands of actors. We see an average of thirty people for a role. If you go in with the attitude, 'Oh, my God, there are twenty-nine other actors here. I don't have a chance,' then you're right—you don't—and you might as well go home." She prefers the alternative reaction. "'Oh, my God, she thinks I'm one of the thirty best in the city for this role. I've already beaten out thousands. My chances are pretty good.'"

She also tells the actor to think of the audition as a performance. "We, as casting directors, probably don't even know what we want. We've got a general idea in our heads, and we're waiting for the actor to come in and show us, perform for us, and that's how we usually make our decisions."

If there is one pet peeve that Benjamin has, it's an actor who fails to listen to direction. After she or the director tells the actor something, the actor will very often continue doing exactly what he or she did before, or do something else altogether. "Because they're usually so busy trying to think of what to say next to impress us, they're not hearing what we've said." And if actors don't listen to direction during an audition, chances are they won't respond on the set either, so there goes the opportunity.

Benjamin prides herself on providing plenty of opportunity to minority actors. For a production of *Romeo and Juliet*, she cast an African-American in the role of Capulet; he was right for the part.

There are certain actors she'll consider for stage productions but not for features. "It's a physical difference," she explains. "There are some actors who can do very nicely on stage, and possibly even on television, but who couldn't make it on film for a variety of reasons, the main one being that some actors haven't learned to control their faces. If they do too much with their facial muscles, it may work on stage, but no one wants to see a rubber face fifteen feet high on the screen, unless it's a real character part."

Eyes are also very important on screen, whereas onstage they're barely noticeable. Can an actor learn to control his or her face? "Absolutely. If you take some kind of on-camera audition course, or even if you have your own video camera, you can monitor yourself."

Benjamin understands the pressures besetting the actor. She herself started out acting, but she opted to take the proverbial path of least resistance. She doesn't think of herself as a failed actor and hopes that actors don't feel they've failed once they've chosen a different pursuit. "Acting, to me," she recalls, "was a carrot dangling out there that I was trying to catch. Once I caught it and started to work regularly, I found I didn't even like it! I spent all day saying someone else's words and all night learning them. I had to get out, because I'd lost *me*. And I really think that's why there are so many actors in this world, because they're all chasing that carrot and don't really want it once they've caught it. And it's okay to walk away from it. It doesn't mean you've failed."

Jack Bowdan

JAY BINDER CASTING

Associates: Jay Binder, Mark Brandon, Amy Kitts
513 West 54th St.
New York, NY 10019
(212) 586-6777
FAX (212) 977-5686

To Jack Bowdan, the most important element in casting is who the actors are as people. That's aside from their preparation, presentation, and theatrical training. "If we don't get a sense of who these people are as individuals, it doesn't mean much, no matter how well prepared they are or what work they're doing."

Jay Binder Casting tries to help actors be themselves by providing as comfortable an environment as possible. Then it's up to each actor. "Actors need to be prepared," stresses Bowdan. "If they come in with prepared material, they need to have spent as much time as necessary with it. Memorization isn't important, but they do need to be familiar with the script. That way," he adds, "they don't get locked into one way of doing something, and they can be open to any adjustments a director may give them." That shows a flexibility and an ability to work in a give-and-take situation. "Most directors," Bowdan believes, "are pretty insecure themselves. They want to come away from an audition knowing that they're going to be able to work with the actor, and that the actor is imaginative enough and well-trained enough to handle different directions. They also need to get a feel for what the actor will be like to work with for an extended period of time."

While Bowdan believes it imperative that an actor reveal who he or she is, it can be carried to extremes. He recalls an episode in which an actor talked herself right out of a part. She apparently had done a lovely audition, and the director was impressed, but afterward she got a bit carried away: "She started chattering

CREDITS INCLUDE:
Proposals Theater
The Last Night of Ballyhoo Theater
Laughter on the 23rd Floor Theater
The King and I (1996) Theater
I'll Fly Away Series
New York News Series

about everything and nothing—and her entire life history—and in about ten minutes totally ruined her chances." The director came to the realization that spending four weeks in rehearsal with this woman was about the last thing he wanted to do.

Training is another important element. Bowdan feels it's less important for television, where personality and physical qualities are primarily the focus, but on the stage actors really need to have training. "A director has to know that the actors can deliver night after night, that they're trained vocally as well as physically to work on the stage." The best young theater actors, he adds, are the ones who come out of such well-known programs as those at Juilliard, Yale, New York University, the University of California at San Diego, and American Conservatory Theatre. One of the wonderful things about these schools, Bowdan explains, is that upon completion of training, actors can be seen in presentations by every casting director and agent in New York and many in Los Angeles. "It's never a guarantee," he admits, "but they have a real head start on other young actors who don't have that kind of training, and those in the theater will respond to that."

Showcases are another source of talent for the Binder Agency. They try to see as many as possible, as long as they are reputable and seem interesting. "Amy Kitts will go to see a Shakespeare showcase, but reluctantly," explains Bowdan, "because they're usually quite terrible, and the actors are not really trained enough to handle the language." She prefers a contemporary play, which allows actors to show themselves off in a better light. "Jay, on the other hand, has this thing against so-called Southern plays," says Bowdan. "They're highly emotional, and there's a lot of bad language and heated stuff going on, and he got so tired of seeing them, he just decided against them."

When they do discover talent, they respond immediately. Bowdan recalls a play called *Love and Magic in Momma's Kitchen*, which the agency was casting for European film director Lina Wertmüller. One of the characters in the play was a sixty-year-old woman dying of cancer. A much younger actress had come in to read for another role but was adamant about reading for the elderly character. She said it was uncanny how much the woman resembled a relative of hers, and she simply had to give it a shot. Her reading was so excellent that the agency brought her back to meet Wertmüller, who ended up casting her.

Some actors mesmerize Bowdan. Mary Louise Parker is one. He was casting *Prelude to a Kiss* at Berkeley Repertory Theatre and thought Mary Louise would be a good choice for one of the leads. He had seen her in other regional theaters, but the director was hesitant to cast an unknown. But it was felt that she was perfect for the part, and after some debate, the director decided to take the chance. Not only did Parker do a superb job at Berkeley, but she went on to do the play in New York and captured a Tony nomination for her performance. "It was her unique qualities: a combination of great skill and technique with an enormous emotional range and a wonderful quirky personality that was very well suited for this particular role."

Bowdan suggests actors keep in touch by sending him an updated picture and résumé every so often, or a postcard if they're appearing in a showcase or production. (But not too many and not too often.) And a final word of advice: All an actor can do is express who he or she is as an individual. "It may not be what's wanted at the time, but it will leave an impression, and that's really all an actor can do."

Jackie Briskey

c/o Casting Society of America
606 N. Larchmont Blvd. #4B
Los Angeles, CA 90004
(213) 463-1925

ention Danielle Steele to Jackie Briskey and you'd think they were family. In fact, Briskey and Steele go back a number of years, but it was NBC, not genetic bonding, that brought them together. Briskey has been responsible for the casting of several Steele projects, including *Family Album*.

It all started when Briskey was teamed with Denise Chamian, but now on her own (their partnership ended), she roams from one studio lot to another, going from assignment to assignment. Considering the twenty years she's been in business, first at MTM, then at Lorimar, and then at Spelling, she is amazingly unassuming and at ease despite her constant state of flux.

"I like what I do," Briskey admits, sitting at her desk piled high with 8 x 10s which she personally peruses. "I look at every single picture that comes into my office. It doesn't matter to me through which agent it comes. If the actor has the right look, I'll bring him or her in, because I've found good people who lacked effective representation." She's been known to find agents for talented actors who've made an impression at a cold reading.

Which brings us to Briskey's advice for actors on that vital subject: "The most important thing an actor should do is be *prepared*," she advises. "If it's a co-starring role or even a nice scene, if you're going to speak intelligently, you've got to read the script." She makes sure that when sides are available prior to a cold reading, a number of scripts are also on hand for the actor to borrow. "I've asked actors many times if they've read the script, and too often they'll say no. Well, that means they didn't take the time, which leaves a sour impression. When an actor is well prepared, even if he or she is wrong for the role, it makes a good impression, and in the future I'll try to find

CREDITS INCLUDE:
On Call Pilot
Yes, Mr. Moon Pilot
Pacific Palisades
Family Album
WKRP in Cincinnati

something right for that actor who has cared enough to be prepared. Even if you don't have much experience, if you've taken the time to read the script, it means a lot."

Briskey assures actors that she, as well as everyone in the audition room, is rooting for them. They all want any actor walking through the door to be good. "This is particularly true for the casting director, because the actor is representing his or her taste, and the biggest compliment we can get is for the producers to turn to us after a session and say, 'They were all good. What do we do?' Then the casting director has done his or her job."

When you come in for a cold reading, it is just that, she says, and that means no props. "It's very distracting. I'm pretty easygoing, but when an actor is reading for others on the team it's critical." Jackie recalls actors coming in with bags full of props, and she feels it just isn't professional. "We have some imagination, you know." That goes for dress, as well. "Dressing close to the role is fine, but if you have five appointments that day, you certainly don't have to change your clothes five times. In other words, if you're reading for the role of an intern, you don't have to go out and get the scrubs."

Another no-no at cold readings: Don't touch the casting director. "I've had people push me up against the wall," Briskey relates. "One time, an actor reading for the part of a mugger came up behind and held a pencil to my throat throughout the entire audition. I couldn't even read with him. He did a good job, but he didn't get the role. One of the reasons, I'm sure, was that the producers and director felt he went a bit too far."

She's told that story over the years to various people, and it apparently came back to that particular actor, who immediately sent Jackie a box of pencils with her name on them. "I called him, and we laughed about it. I'm sure he learned his lesson."

Other actors, Briskey cautions, talk themselves out of a job. "They'll remind producers or directors that they'd met at a party a long time ago. That's embarrassing to a producer who can't recall every actor he or she has run into. Just come in, ask questions, discuss the role, and read. If you feel you can do the reading better, ask to do it again. In and out. It's okay to be cordial and friendly, but if you have to spend fifteen minutes reminding someone who you are, it's better left unsaid."

The best way to stay fresh in Briskey's memory is to appear in a theatrical production or showcase. She's an avid theatergoer and will attend reputable showcases. "The best ones are those that have names attached to them. You get to know different acting coaches and the ones who are good. I attend showcases that screen their actors and have good taste in whom they choose." She suggests networking with other actors or your agent to come up with some worthwhile workshops. Briskey says Cynthia Ettinger was one actress who made the right selection: "I happened to go to a showcase to see someone I already knew, and there was this young lady I thought was exceptional. She had no agent, no manager, no nothing. I called her in to read and brought her to my producers, who agreed she was wonderful, and she wound up with a regular role on a series." In a matter of two weeks, Ettinger went from showcase to network.

An important addendum: Make sure you showcase yourself properly. "I've found, in a lot of cases, that actors cast themselves in the wrong roles," Briskey warns. "If you're a good-looking guy and take on a character part, or you do comedy when your comedy's not that strong, it doesn't put you in the best light." She also recommends that an actor stick as close to his or her age range as possible.

Acting classes are another tool for the actor. "It's imperative that someone who wants to do TV take classes that teach camera. Camera classes will help stage actors get used to working in front of the lens." Other helpful classes can improve your scene study, cold reading, and improvisation skills. "Acting classes are the best place for learning and exposure. Audit a class. If the coach won't let you sit in on a session, something's wrong. You need to see if the class is one you can identify with. There are so many styles of teaching, and different actors respond to different things." Once you've found a coach you feel you can work with, sign up and stick with it.

Don't, however, stick with headshots that don't look like you—that's one of Briskey's commandments. "What's irritating to me is actors using photos that are five or even ten years old. If actors walk in and look totally different from their pictures, it's not fair. I'm not talking about a different haircut or even a different hair color. I just want it to be a good representation of what you look like."

Briskey says she likes actors. While she herself has never wanted to act, she respects those who do, and especially those who work at their craft. "I've read that Joanne Woodward still takes classes. If *she* does, then there isn't an actor on this earth who shouldn't continue learning."

Ross Brown

BROWN/WEST & COMPANY

Partner: Mary West
7319 Beverly Blvd. #10
Los Angeles, CA 90036
(213) 938-2575
FAX (213) 938-2755

Television, movies, miniseries—Brown/West has done them all, and Ross Brown himself has been doing it for over a quarter of a century. In Brown's opinion, the hardest thing about being an actor is not doing the job but *getting* the job—something most actors haven't been adequately trained to do. Brown has seen many actors with talent fall by the wayside because of their lack of savvy when it comes to auditioning. "It's all seduction," he believes. An actor should never give his or her all during the first reading, but only a taste of what he has to offer: "Once you've seen it all, are you going to buy it? It's an art form, and it requires a professional approach."

Aside from talent and presence, Brown believes the basics for an actor are courtesy, integrity, and a sense of humor. He prides himself on his ability to help prepare actors to get jobs. "I'll basically give them choices as to what we want and different areas to which they can go. I'll even tell them what to wear! They're there to get the job. What I would love is that they would all go in there and *take* the job." The more special an actor is to him, the more he tries to help, although he wants the actor to understand that no matter how good he or she may be, it's not always the best actor who lands the role. There are too many variables in this elusive business.

The actors who break through are "not the pretty girls or handsome boys, but the trendsetters—they have a uniqueness that makes you not just want to look at them, but *see* them." One such individual is Randy Quaid. Brown found him in Houston when he was casting the

CREDITS INCLUDE:
Halloween 6
Sister Island
Petals in the Wind
The Last Picture Show
Woman on a Ledge
The Morris Dees Story
The Fire Next Time
North & South, Book Two

now-classic *The Last Picture Show*. It was Quaid's first film. What was so special about him? "You cared about him. If you don't care, my favorite four-letter word is *next!*"

Another actor made such an impression on Brown that he searched the world to find him. It was Rutger Hauer, whom he'd seen in the Dutch film *Soldier of Orange*. Casting the miniseries *Inside the Third Reich*, the story of Albert Speer, Brown thought Hauer would be perfect for the lead. "They wanted William Hurt, and while I'm a big fan of Hurt, I was convinced we should track down Hauer, even though he wasn't a big name at the time." After finding the European actor and reading him, the producers agreed. He was the choice.

Brown may be extremely polite to certain actors, but that doesn't mean he favors them. "I'm looking for people you write scripts for. I'm extremely polite to people I intend not to see again. But if there's someone I think has potential and isn't using it, I'll nail him to the bloody wall!" In other words, if you're read the riot act in Brown's office, you've probably landed the role. He doesn't have time to get angry at those with little talent or those he terms "hungry" actors. "You don't give a hungry people filet mignon. You give them Alpo—a whole case of it."

Brown doesn't mince words. He's also a master of expressive analogies. "I feel that all actors are defense attorneys. Their client is their character, and whether they're playing Lizzie Borden or Adolf Hitler, their responsibility is to make the audience, which is the jury, believe they're innocent. The minute actors believe their clients are guilty, they lose, and so do we." What saddens him most about the business are the people who have forgotten to "make believe." Imagination, one of the magical qualities of show business, he says, is lacking in many individuals.

Another attribute he finds lacking in many actors is the ability to listen. "The most important thing to acting is listening and reacting to what you've heard. You have to listen to what is being said, digest it, and spit out what you don't need. But what you hear and like is yours." Brown himself is a good listener. In fact, he prefers to listen to actors rather than hear them read when he first meets them. "I'd rather listen to what they have to say. I'm not really that big on readings." And when he does schedule readings they're usually with the producers and director. "I try to set up as few callbacks as possible."

What exactly is he looking for? "I never know what I want until they come in. I've had to cast roles written for men and realized a woman would be better." A case in point was *Intimate Agonies*, set in a very WASP environment. In one hospital scene, there was a call for a gruff redneck physician in his fifties. So whom did Brown call in to read for this character? Two black women, and one was cast. "When it comes to filling a role, number one is the human being, number two is the human being who's either a male or female, and number three is the human being who's a male or female who's also a doctor."

What's most important to Brown in the casting of a film is the whole "canvas": "The star is the color red, let's say. Then I'll add different colors that will work with red and make that actor look the best. I may find a wonderful blue, but that blue doesn't work on my canvas. That's why an actor shouldn't feel bad when he or she doesn't get the role. It may just be a case of being just the wrong match for that particular canvas."

Brown isn't afraid to seek out new or untried actors. In fact, he and his partner, Mary West, have vowed to use a client from a new agency on every project in which they're involved. Not too long ago, Brown found an actor in Dallas with no professional experience. He'd just come along with a friend to a casting session. "He was a real winner, a bigger-than-life character. So I called the William Morris Agency, and they signed him. He wasn't even a member of SAG." Almost immediately after landing an agent, that fine young actor, Thomas Hayden Church, was cast in the TV series *Wings*.

Of course, being without a union card doesn't necessarily mean that an actor hasn't been well trained. "Training is important," Brown emphasizes. "Smart actors, even when they're doing a series or whatever, will study, because that's where they find their new bags of tricks." He cites the numerous actors who disappear from view soon after their series is dropped from the lineup. He feels it's because they haven't done their homework. What he would like actors to keep in mind is that casting directors are subjective like everyone else. "We're simply buyers. The minute we buy you, we immediately have to sell you. But we can often sell you better than you can yourself." And if he's not buying for one reason or another, it's not because you're not talented or you're not a terrific person. "It's just not our story. It has nothing to do with the story we're currently working on, so I simply have to say, *next!*"

Denise Chamian

DENISE CHAMIAN CASTING

4113 Radford Ave
Studio City, CA 91604
(818) 754-5404
FAX (818) 754-5405

Working out of her current office in West Los Angeles, Denise Chamian reflects on her work casting Steven Spielberg's *Saving Private Ryan.* As a woman about town—she moves from one location and project to another—she maintains a relaxed demeanor. "I've been fortunate," she says, "to work for some incredibly talented and nice casting directors, like Jackie Briskey, Reuben Cannon, Jane Jenkins, and Janet Hirshenson. They've taught me that it's our responsibility to come in and do a good job, always keeping in mind that we should treat actors with respect, be nice to them, and have fun."

Chamian found her niche when she discovered casting after a brief stint with a theatrical agency, and the feeling is obviously mutual: When producers discover Chamian, they give her repeat business. (Clients include Aaron Spelling; Keith Samples, at Rysher Entertainment; Dennis Hammer, at NBC; and Papazian–Hirsch).

"What I try to do as a casting director," she explains, "is be as accessible and as kind to actors as I can. It's not possible to be there for them at every moment, but I try to promote a sense of working together."

She also likes to see as many new faces as she can under her limited time constraints; she looks at every submission that comes across her desk, solicited or not. "I have no A or B pile. Photos I don't want are picked up by Your Picture Service (a headshot recycling service) and returned to the actors. It makes me crazy to see actors throwing away all those pictures." Although the actor in question must pay for such delivery service, Chamian notes that it only costs about a dime a picture.

When it comes to videos, however, she'll

CREDITS INCLUDE:
Saving Private Ryan
Mystic Pizza
Mouse Hunt
High Incident
The Invaders

only see those sent in by agents. She prefers strictly theatrical reels: "I like to see reels that display an actor's range. I don't want to see commercial pieces unless they're the only clips you have. I like to see different types of roles, and I like to see only legitimate jobs on the tape, no simulated scenes or monologues. A screen test is okay if it's very good." Keep it short, she adds—between three and ten minutes—and make sure it's the best representation of your work.

Although this casting director works mainly with agents, she doesn't limit her contacts only to those at the top. Chamian says she'll lend an ear to any agent who may have the next rising star. "They help find the new talent, and once I've contacted Breakdown Services, I'll talk to any agent who feels they represent the right choices." After all, with the growing volume of talent in town today, Chamian admits she needs all the help she can get. "It's overwhelming. And not everyone—those with agents included—has talent. There are a lot of people out there who aren't qualified to be actors who get representation by those not qualified to be agents."

The onus is on the casting director to weed through the undiscovered talent, trying to find the latest and greatest. Although Chamian shies away from citing specific actors whom she's discovered, she does admit to giving Brad Pitt two lines on *Trial and Error,* a 1986 sitcom she cast. Matthew Perry was another novice she cast early on. So what was it about these future stars that caught her attention?

"There's something about their being, the aura around them," Chamian answers. "They stand out from everyone—it was like Bruce Willis on *Moonlighting,* which I helped cast. When I first met Bruce I said, 'Wow!' You could just feel his presence in the room. He wasn't the average actor."

Unfortunately, she says, discovering talent is a subjective process, and opinions can vary widely. For example, Chamian notes that she has been a fan of actor Viggo (*The Prophecy*) Mortenson's for years—but it is only recently that industry execs have concurred with her vision. "I kept telling producers about Viggo; I told them they had to meet this guy. Nobody picked up on him, and today he's headed for superstardom. Finally, somebody gets it and gives him a part, and there you go!"

If there is a notable casting trend today, she adds, it's that everyone seems to be newly interested in the art. "Even those not in the industry are now paying attention to casting. More producers and directors are able to recognize good acting when they see it." She thinks it may have something to do with the greater numbers of actors being seen and the obvious difference between the wheat and the chaff.

And speaking of sorting out the quality submissions, Chamian notes that she is wary of the advertised services that promise to get an actor's headshot out to all the agents and casting directors. She adds that she's never brought in a single actor from such a service. "It smacks of ripping off actors. Agents have reputations and training, and they're the ones who should be sending the pictures out and soliciting actors. Sending masses of pictures with nothing specific in mind doesn't make sense to me."

As for showcases, although Chamian used to participate occasionally, she no longer has the time or inclination to be involved. "I was feeling guilty not bringing in those actors who paid to meet me, so I found myself bringing in the best of the worst. I didn't feel a lot of them were particularly good, so I stopped doing it."

Chamian admits she's had a few offers to go in front of the camera herself—something she's never considered seriously. Her words of wisdom for actors: Do the job well, and do it simply. Just come in and read without extraneous props or shtick. "It's tough to be an actor," she notes. "And my heart goes out to you all. That's why I try to make the process as easy as possible."

Aleta Chappelle

F.D. PRODUCTIONS, INC.

250 W. 57th St. #1516
New York, NY 10107
(212) 642-6355

Aleta Chappelle started out casting extras for such acclaimed films as *The Cotton Club* and *Ironweed*. She loved the work and spent as much time finding the right people for nonspeaking roles as many casting directors spend on principals. Her technique? "You get thousands of people in, and you pick out the really unique ones." She would devote about thirty seconds to each person, accepting the potential actor's picture and résumé and asking a few basic questions. "Then, if there were someone who seemed especially nice or serious, someone who just looked right, I'd put his or her picture in my special box, and later on, as we set up readings, we'd bring them in." In other words, just because someone had always done extra work didn't necessarily mean that the actor wouldn't be considered for a speaking part.

Chappelle saw six thousand people during open calls for both *The Cotton Club* and *Ironweed*. The calls were always announced in the local papers, and anyone was welcome to attend. In Albany, New York, on-location for the latter film, she recalls casting one man who was an alderman; he wound up playing a bum and working four or five weeks. "SAG was really mad at us, because it was such an important part, and we'd given it to a nonprofessional." She also hired a woman who was head of the Albany arts council to play a floozy. But one of Chappelle's favorite stories was the casting of a homeless family. "There was a scene where Jack Nicholson is supposed to give some food to a husband, wife, and baby who are totally indigent, and we got a real family to do this. They were in a situation where they lived above a store with about twenty other people. They didn't even qualify for welfare, and suddenly they became principal weekly players, earning five thousand dollars with a

CREDITS INCLUDE:
The Nutty Professor
Three Wishes
Losing Isaiah
Sister Act 2
Godfather 3

chance to turn their lives around." Nicholson himself was captivated by one homeless man, and the actor insisted the man be upgraded to a principal. "He was the only person that Jack gave an autograph to during the shoot," Chappelle remembers.

Even though she no longer focuses on atmosphere casting, she still spends a lot of time looking for special faces in the crowd. Even Francis Ford Coppola, she reveals, will meet actors who may not have any dialogue but whose faces may be on camera for several seconds, or whose action may require more skill than is usual for the average extra.

While casting *A Rage in Harlem,* Chappelle went to Cincinnati to do some location casting. There she found an ex–football player at an open call. At two other open calls, she was searching not only for day players but for the female lead to play opposite Forrest Whitaker. Robin Givens ultimately got the role, but two women with no experience were also given screen tests. In other words, the motto "Once an extra, always an extra" does not hold true for Chappelle. "I think it's a good way to learn filmmaking. If it's what you do for a living, then you're probably going to stay an extra, because people are going to look at you that way. But if you're a young person or new to the business and really want to get some experience, I don't think it hurts."

Chappelle believes casting is 80 to 90 percent based on an actor's looks and attitude, especially in film. "That's why I always like to meet an actor first. My favorite people have something in their personality, or there's something they bring in that's real." There are times she won't even read an actor until the callbacks and taping sessions. This is most common when she's already familiar with the work of an actor. For example, John Hurt played a major part in the film *Rambling Rose* but never read for it. However, Chris Sarandon, whom she'd previously cast in *True Believers,* was auditioned, because he wanted to play the part of an older doctor, which was a stretch.

Although Chappelle may prefer hiring an actor who fits the part physically, that's not to say she doesn't respect training. "Training is important. It legitimizes our seriousness. I think it's great to see people coming out of Juilliard. I always give them a break, because they went through more." And the more you work, the better, she believes, even if it's doing student films. "They aren't true filmmaking, but they do give you a lot of experience." She cites the case of Robert Burke, who beat out some heavyweight names for a major part in *Rambling Rose.* A friend of his apparently talked him into doing a student project in New York. That piece of film wound up in Chappelle's hands, and Burke's career was launched.

Chappelle also advocates furthering one's general education: "Cultivate writing, cultivate dance. I think some of the people who are most interesting are those who are well rounded. People should work on being a whole person. That makes you a better actor."

She cautions actors against unscrupulous agents. "There are so-called agencies that I think are a big farce, really insulting, and sad. Every time I go into a small town, I see these corrupt agencies where they make people spend thousands on their stupid classes and photographs, and the actors think they're doing something when it's usually just the agent making money off them." A better approach is to study, work, and constantly send out pictures to agents. That's one of the things she appreciates about the American casting system. In Europe, she says, actors don't have 8 x 10s to send to casting directors. In fact, they're insulted if someone calls them in for an audition. "In Italy, you simply sit and have a cappu-cino with an actor you're considering for a film, and if you want a picture you may be presented with a 2 x 1-foot portrait!"

"8 x 10s, *si!* Postcards, *no!*" Chappelle hates picture postcards. Expressing an attitude quite different from the majority of casting directors, she believes the postcard "classifies you as an extra." Another word of warning: If an actor is not in the *Players' Guide*, he or she is making a big mistake. "I think the actors' books are impor-tant. It's very convenient for us. I had many late-night calls on *God-father*, where I had to use those books literally at the last minute."

Not getting anywhere fast? "Stick with it," advises Chappelle. "I don't think acting is the worst job in the world. It's one of the hard-est things you can choose but I think if you work as much as you can, it can only make you better."

Lori Cobe-Ross

2005 Palo Verde Ave. #306
Long Beach, CA 90815
(562) 596-7406

Lori Cobe-Ross enjoys casting low-budget films because she has much more autonomy than she would have if the budgets were over $9 million. The same holds true for syndicated-television versus network programming. "It's a lot of casting by committee there," says Cobe-Ross of network operations. "If you do a sitcom, and you have someone who has one line, you have to bring in twenty people to a bunch of producers who basically sit there and say, 'He's not funny.'"

Working on smaller-scale productions, Cobe-Ross pretty much calls the shots. For instance, *Wake, Rattle and Roll* called for a punk genie, and observing that there hadn't been many women on the show, Cobe-Ross called the producers and suggested casting a woman. Presto change-o! "Now, can you imagine a network altering the script like that?" She had much the same power on the feature *Body Shot,* where she was able to cast the two leads. At Paramount or Sony, the stars are usually set before the casting director is even hired.

It's not so much the power as the challenge that is so attractive to Cobe-Ross. "I like having actors come in and read. I'd love to see fifty people for each role if I could." Even after all her years of casting, she never tires of meeting new people and discovering new talent. In fact, Cobe-Ross has a reputation as being one of the nicest casting directors in town. "I just try to make the actors feel really comfortable, because I figure, if they're comfortable, they're going to be able to give me their best performance."

In her opinion, an actor at an audition should complete his or her reading before chatting with the casting director. "I don't want them to get distracted, so I say 'Let's read first, and then we can talk.'" She also encourages actors to ask as many questions about the script or character as necessary. If a scene calls for some kind of business—making coffee,

CREDITS INCLUDE:
Confessions
Time Shifters
Body Shot
Monsoon
Divorce Court

for instance—she would like the actor to ask if he or she should mime this or simply ignore it. "I don't think there are any stupid questions, I really don't." Cobe-Ross is also one of the few people in her field who believes in telling actors if they've done well. "And, if I'm sure I'm going to call someone back, I'll say so."

Although it's not possible to keep every photo and résumé that comes across her desk, she does go through them all, sorting them by character. When it comes time to cast a specific role, she looks through her files, determining if the look is right and then checking the actor's credits. She won't hesitate to cast an inexperienced actor for a minor role, but she rarely takes chances on a featured character. There are occasional exceptions. Cobe-Ross saw Scott Thompson Baker on *Star Search*. Two and a half years later, Baker's manager pitched him for a role in a film Cobe-Ross was casting. She assumed that Scott had been working steadily since this "discovery" and was amazed he hadn't had a real break. Despite his lack of experience, she believed Scott could do the job and hired him. Not only did he succeed in that role, he went on to greater success as a regular on *General Hospital*.

A strong concern with minority casting stems from her association with one director in particular, Jag Mundhra, with whom she's done five or six films. He's always aware of the possibility of casting a minority actor, and he made her aware of it early on.

Even though the budgets she works with aren't monster-sized, they are significant, and it's rare that Cobe-Ross has hired a nonunion actor. On *Divorce Court*, she occasionally was able to hire someone on the basis of the 1941 Taft-Hartley Act, which allows a performer who appears on camera for the first time and has at least one word of dialogue to become eligible to join Screen Actors Guild. She recalls one episode that called for a wrestler. She didn't know many wrestling actors, and when one came along who impressed her with his reading, she hired him without a card. "I don't do nonunion films, however," she says, "because I don't know any nonunion actors."

She believes that an experienced actor has developed a technique that's vital to his or her career. "You have to develop some kind of on-camera technique. You can tell when you see someone on TV if he or she is experienced or not. You can feel it." But if someone is really good despite a lack of experience, she may talk to the director and get the actor in to read.

Cobe-Ross certainly doesn't want to suggest that it's easy for inexperienced actors to break into the business. She often feels it would be beneficial for actors to be required to work in a casting office for at least a week. "Once they see what the odds are of getting a job, then they should make a decision: If they *still* want to act, they deserve to. However, if they say, 'Oh God, how am I ever going to compete?' that should be the determining factor."

Should an actor opt to pursue the craft, Cobe-Ross has this piece of advice: Relax. "The thing I find most comforting," she relates, "is when someone comes in who's relaxed—maybe because, if they're nervous, it makes me feel uncomfortable for them." She suggests a calm and prepared demeanor. She also likes an actor to take chances. "If it's too big, I can always say, 'Bring it down a little.' But if someone comes in and gives this flat, boring reading, I'm just going to say 'thank you' and lead him or her to the door."

Another attribute that impresses Cobe-Ross is training. "I'd say, number one, you have to study." Her sister learned this lesson the hard way. She had begged Cobe-Ross for an opportunity to read for a role for which she was sure she was perfect. She had no experience but wanted to be an actress. "I said, 'Fine, come in and read,' and I had the director here. Well, I never heard a word about acting from her since. She just didn't realize it was so hard."

Training and experience are why Cobe-Ross likes an actor to do as much theater and as many showcases as possible. She even helps actors refine their skills at cold-reading workshops in Los Angeles and Orange counties. "I'm a frustrated teacher," she confesses. "I love doing this, but I also realize what teachers earn." At her workshops she'll meet actors, pair them up, have them read the sides she's selected, critique them or give them direction, and have them do it again. She's even hired actors through these workshops. "Casting directors are desperate to find good talent, and I'll go anywhere I can."

If you're going to be in a showcase or in a theatrical production, Lori Cobe-Ross wants to hear from you. Not by phone, of course, but by postcard. It's virtually impossible for her to see every play in town, but if your timing's right, you may luck out!

Eric Dawson

ULRICH/DAWSON/KRITZER CASTING

Associates: Robert Ulrich, Carol Kritzer
3151 Cahuenga Blvd. West, Suite 310
Los Angeles, CA 90068
(213) 845-1100
FAX (213) 845-1101

Eric Dawson likes actors. He's married to an actress, as is his partner Robert Ulrich. "I think our office is particularly actor-friendly," he admits, "and that's why I want to stress to actors that acting is a business, and that along with studying and all that other important stuff, you also need to work on your business skills." In the ten years he's had his own company, he has seen many actors fall by the wayside because of a lack of business acumen.

"You have to do your homework," he stresses. "One of my biggest complaints is that actors don't even know what's on TV. They come in to read for an episodic show and say they've never seen the show or don't own a television." He believes that if you want to work in television, you should know what it's about. "If you're auditioning for, say, *The Gregory Hines Show,* it has a very different feel from *Home Boys in Outer Space,* and to have never seen the shows or gotten an idea who the characters are certainly won't help you." He adds that actors gain at least a ten-percent advantage of getting the job if they have a feel for the show, even if they've only seen it once. "A casting director can provide only a little background on a character before the audition, and if an actor has prepared the material with the wrong take and suddenly finds he or she has misinterpreted the character, that actor's obviously not going to do the best job."

While Dawson won't admit to being uninterested in actors who don't watch his shows, he makes it clear that he's influenced on that score when making his final decision. "When people come in and say, 'This show takes place in New

CREDITS INCLUDE:
Early Edition
The Dave Chappelle Project Pilot
Anne Rice's Rag & Bone Pilot
The Gregory Hines Show
Dark Skies
Perry Mason TV movies

Orleans, do you want an accent? I didn't prepare one,' our response is: 'Why not? And why didn't you call your agent and get that information before you came here?'"

Other annoyances to Dawson are actors who come to an audition with the wrong sides. "Our office is very good. We'll even fax sides to agents. There's no excuse for having the wrong material. How can you show yourself at your best if all of a sudden you have to run out, grab two more pages, and read them cold?"

It's equally annoying to him when actors hand him old résumés that haven't been updated and tell him it's their agent's fault. "It may be your agent's responsibility, but it's your career," he warns. "And if you know your agent has faxed us your photo, make sure you have a hard copy with you when you go into a producer session. These are things that give you that little bit of an advantage. "

A disadvantage to actors springs from bringing props to auditions. Dawson does not appreciate having a gun pulled on him during a reading or having an actor get physical with him. "We've had that happen. I'm there to watch you act, and when you pull me into your scene in front of the producer, not only can I not see you objectively, but all of a sudden the producers are watching me half the time. It just doesn't make sense." He also discourages costumes. "If you're coming in for a cop role, you don't need a uniform. I think people associate actors who do that with bit players." He feels that because actors who dress in costume appear more desperate to win the role, it works against them more often than not.

The pressures of casting an episodic TV show require Dawson and his partners to limit the time they can give actors at an audition. "It gets frustrating. You're sitting here praying that the next person is the one you're looking for. We're always down to the wire, especially on a pilot, and we usually finish casting a few days before the shoot." Therefore, when an actor takes up too much time with chit-chat that isn't pertinent, it's counterproductive. "I wish more actors would just come in, be pleasant, ask a question if it's necessary, read and be done with it." Too many actors want to entertain. The problem is time. "Actors will come in, make jokes, rewrite scenes, ask for three takes. I only wish they could read the room better." He suggests that actors notice the reaction of the producers. If there's resistance the first time the actor asks to redo the scene, then why request a third stab at it? Again, he says, it makes the actor look desperate.

"Desperation is apparent in those actors who constantly make excuses and apologize for what they did, even if what they did was great. If an actor questions his or her performance, so will the producers." Then there's the actor who ends the audition by saying, "Well, that's the best I can do with the material. Who wrote this?" And the writer is sitting in the room. "Years ago you didn't have the writer in the room during an audition. In the last ten years it's become commonplace. Chances are, given a writer's insecurity, you're going to insult him or her."

Things have changed in Hollywood, according to Dawson. With the advent of cable stations and syndicated television, there's more product and, thus, a greater need for actors. He finds that actors today are sent out on many more calls per day by their agents. "Actors today have more choices, so that when a better opportunity comes up, they'll cancel the less desirable audition at the last minute. That's one of my biggest pet peeves. If you're given a slot by a casting director to come to a producer session, you're perhaps one of four actors. If we find out at the last minute you aren't coming, all of a sudden we're in a big bind. We try to keep the numbers low to give everybody a better chance, but when we start having a whole bunch of cancellations, we're forced to overload the casting sessions, making everybody more crazy in the long run."

There are instances, however, when a casting director (or his or her office) may be responsible for an error. In one case, which worked out well for all concerned, Dawson was casting an episode for which they were seeking a good-looking man in his early thirties. He gave his assistant a list of people he thought would be appropriate. The assistant apparently got one actor's name confused with another and brought in a fifty-five-year-old character actor as part of the group. "Suddenly I realized the mix-up, but I didn't have the heart to send him home after he'd gone to the trouble of preparing the scene and driving over here. I decided I'd just let him do his thing. The guy reads, and when he leaves I look over at the producers expecting a 'What were you thinking?' look. Instead I get accolades on my brilliant idea. I didn't say anything of course. I just took the credit."

Eric Dawson is grateful to actors who express their appreciation by sending thank-you notes. "Gifts sort of make me uncomfortable, because most of the people who send them can't really afford to. But a thank-you note is always nice if you know we've really fought for you. Casting can be a thankless job, and it's nice to know that when you're in somebody's corner, that person appreciates it. It just lets me know it's recognized."

Lou DiGiaimo

Associates: Brett Goldstein, Lou DiGiaimo, Jr.
513 W. 54th St.
New York, NY 10019
(212) 713-1884
FAX (212) 977-9509

Ridley Scott, Barry Levinson, and William Friedkin have consistently relied on the expertise of Lou DiGiaimo, a truly bicoastal casting director. Although these directors have very different ways of working, DiGiaimo seems to be able to adapt successfully to each of their styles. Levinson, he says, likes to see a bunch of actors for each role, while Scott and Friedkin prefer a narrower selection. DiGiaimo himself feels it's a casting director's duty to pare down the list of potential candidates. He believes any secretary can accumulate a large group of actors to bring to a director, but it's the function of a casting director to separate the wheat from the chaff.

Levinson, he says, requires a broader selection only because he works in comedy, which is more difficult to cast. "Some actors who appear to be funny at first meeting aren't as funny when presented with the material at hand. Comedy takes a special blend of acting ability and an innate humor." DiGiaimo tries to pepper his theatrical outings with occasional comedy club visits, but he confesses that, because there is so much theater in New York, it's difficult to find time to explore other venues. He feels that actors are doing themselves an injustice by not appearing onstage every chance they get. He realizes it's easier in New York, because there are more theatrical outlets in that city. "I would advise any actor starting out to spend time in New York. In fact, I tell actors who move to Los Angeles to come back to New York at least once or twice a year to stay grounded." He quotes Al Pacino, whom he overheard giving advice to another actor not too long ago: "Why are you going to L.A.? Don't you know the sun numbs your brain?" DiGiaimo says most actors in New York are so dedicated they'll create a project

CREDITS INCLUDE:
G.I. Jane
Sleepers
Donnie Brasco
Thelma & Louise
The Godfather
Homicide

among themselves. "Even if they're going to each other's apartments and reading, that's training. That's working at your craft."

He realizes that many Los Angeles actors are reluctant to commit to theater not because they don't want to perform onstage, but because they're afraid they won't be seen by agents and casting directors. Casting directors on the West Coast, he believes, rely less on theater for finding new talent than on film and television, simply because there's less of it.

DiGiaimo tries to see as many actors as he can when he's involved in a project. "I'll see as many as time allows, and I don't care about credits." Brad Pitt didn't have credits when he came in for a reading for *Thelma & Louise*. "We had almost set Billy Baldwin," DiGiaimo explains, "but Business Affairs kept wavering until it was too late, and Baldwin got the lead in *Backdraft*. So I had to start searching." He went to Los Angeles, where he saw at least three hundred actors, including George Clooney and Brad Pitt. "Ridley Scott had already started shooting the film, and we still hadn't found our actor. I brought Brad to him, and though he admired his talent, he thought he might be too young." A week later DiGiaimo brought him back to Scott, who agreed Pitt was the perfect choice.

DiGiaimo will fight for actors with whom he's impressed. He'll make every effort to obtain a meeting with the director, even if the director may be reluctant. When he was doing *Good Morning, Vietnam*, he immediately thought of Forrest Whitaker, who had previously made an impression on him in *The Color of Money*. Levinson didn't feel Whitaker was physically right for the part, but DiGiaimo insisted. "At first he just read for Barry and me, and he was fabulous. But when he thought he'd be reading with Robin Williams at the callback, he was very nervous, and the reading was not good at all." Fortunately, Robin was out of town then, and when he did show up for the third audition, Forrest had gotten over his case of the jitters and landed the role.

DiGiaimo loves finding new, untapped talent off-off-Broadway, through agents, or even in neighborhood schools, as in the case of Joe Perino. "Joe was thirteen when we were casting *Sleepers*. We were searching for kids at a school in the Bronx, and Joe came in. He really wanted to be an actor, and he was great. He'd never acted before." DiGiaimo is also thrilled with finding six-year-old John Luke Figueroa, whom he cast in the Sidney Lumet remake of *Gloria*. Without any credits, young John was able to handle the second lead in a major film.

While a long list of credits isn't vital to DiGiaimo, following direction is. At an audition, if an actor doesn't listen to the casting director or the director, there won't be a callback. "If an actor doesn't agree with an interpretation of the character or has a question about it, let him ask me about it before he reads. But once we ask him for a change, we expect him to make it, not simply ignore the direction." What will happen on the set when the camera is rolling?—that's what worries a director about an actor who ignores suggestions. He or she needs to be assured that an actor is flexible and understands the nature of the character.

DiGiaimo prefers feature film casting to television casting, although he's enjoying *Homicide*, the Barry Levinson series for which he cast the pilot and (as this book goes to press) the guest leads. The day players, he says, are cast out of Baltimore, where it's shot. He'll see actors in New York and send the videotape to the director in Baltimore. "What I don't like about television," he explains, "is that, for me, it's much more political than film, in that there are so many more people involved in the decision-making process. In film there's me, the director, and maybe the producer. In television there's the network brass and all the creative types. I have less control."

DiGiaimo advises actors to get an agent who believes in them—"one who is going to work for you. It doesn't have to be a big agent. And remember, agents don't get you the part. You get the part. The agent gets you through the door." He admits acting is one of the toughest professions you can choose, but if you choose it, you have to persevere. An actor should constantly be working at his or her craft and, eventually, with a little "luck," it will happen."

Pam Dixon

PAM DIXON CASTING

Box 672
Beverly Hills, CA 90213
(310) 271-8064
FAX (310) 271-8430

Pam Dixon doesn't read actors, she meets them. The only time she'll do a reading is when a director is on location and won't be able to meet an actor personally. The readings are usually done when an actor meets with the director, and Dixon says she's able, generally, to tell if actors will be able to handle the material without pre-reading them. "It's instinct; it's different ways to play a role. I don't know that somebody is always right or always wrong. I think you pick qualified actors, and they do the part."

And directors believe in the "Dixon Instinct." During the first week of auditions for *The Craft,* she ran across a young actor named Skeet Ulrich, from New York. "I put him on tape, and four months later when they still hadn't cast the part, I asked them to take another look at Skeet on video. The studio thought he was fantastic, so I called him and said: 'You're not going to believe this, but I'd like you to fly out here and meet the producer.' He did, and he got the role."

What's interesting about that story, she says, is that tape is hardly the best way to go for an audition; yet, if she had not taped that particular audition, Ulrich would never have gotten the part. "So sometimes it's a very useful tool. I was able to pull this out of the proverbial hat at the last minute." Another actor who unexpectedly landed a role in *The Craft* was Robin Tunney, also a New Yorker. "We were film testing here in L.A., and I called Robin to come out and read with the girls trying out for the lead," Dixon explains. "I told her she could even play the supporting role herself, and that she might get it if she did well. Well, we showed the test to the studio, and they turned to me and said,

CREDITS INCLUDE:
Mighty Joe Young
Zorro
My Giant
Afterglow
Waterdance
Angels in the Outfield

'You know what? We love Robin Tunney.' And we brought her out again and tested her, not for the part she'd read for, but for the lead. And she got it!"

Dixon prefers bringing in three or four choices for every role, each providing a totally different way of playing the part. She also enjoys casting against type and looking for unusual choices. Depending on the project, she'll even cast nonactors, like author Tom Robbins or musicians Neil Young and Tom Petty. She's even been responsible for a script change due to an unusual casting choice. For *City Slickers*, she was asked to find two dentists. Not only did she find two black actors to portray the dentists, but because of their age difference, in a rewrite they became father and son.

Dixon works primarily with agents, although when it comes to casting children, she'll venture into unknown territory. When she was looking for kids for *Baby Boom*, she scheduled an open call at the Los Angeles County Museum, where she saw 1,500 little ones from 8:30 A.M. to 6 P.M. She'll also broaden her search when she needs to expand her horizons. Such was the case with *Zorro*, which she cast for Steven Spielberg. "I must have seen over a thousand actors for the two young leads. I saw every Hispanic actress, model, and singer around, whether they were submitted by agents or whether they sent me a headshot on their own." They eventually cast a relatively unknown actress to play the female lead and a complete unknown for the lieutenant.

Another relatively unknown actor whom Dixon helped "put on the map" was a young man who'd just had a small role in *Dazed and Confused* and was referred to Dixon by the producer of that film. "This friend of mine knew I was casting *Angels in the Outfield*, and knew I was looking for an actor who could play baseball. He said this actor was a college ball player and was really good. I told him to send him right over. I tested him on the spot. The director never even met him, and he landed the role. The young man was Matthew McConaughey. He went from working for scale to making a million dollars on his next film, *A Time to Kill*."

Dixon enjoys finding actors in the theater. When she does, she says she's rarely concerned about their ability to make the transition to film. "Most of the actors I've met have not taken any special camera courses, and most of them have made the transition very well." She's opposed to actors paying a lot of money for workshops. "There's a history of people being paid to attend workshops; I do not attend them. The actors who pay all this money for these courses are actors who really can ill afford it." She will, however, go to non-Equity showcases and encourage actors to try to get into these or other small theater groups so that casting directors like herself can see their work—"especially today," she stresses." Almost all the casting directors really do pay attention to the theater, because it's gotten so good in the past few years that it really is worthwhile."

The most important concern to Dixon is that actors come to an audition prepared. "They should get their sides early enough to be familiar with them, and if they have questions, they should ask ahead of time. They can even call the office or ask their agent to call me if they want to know how I or the director sees the character." Actors, she adds, should be aware that most directors don't want to chat at length at auditions. "They just want to get into it, and I think if you want to chat, you should wait until the reading is over. It saves your concentration. When people start talking and thinking about other things, their concentration is lessened somewhat." Dixon advises against apologies if an actor isn't satisfied with the reading. "If you don't think you've done well, take the casting director aside and say, 'I really didn't feel good about that. I'd like to come back again, if I may.'" Saying something negative in front of a director, she believes, may hurt an actor's chances, because the director may not have felt the reading was that bad.

She tells her students in the two-year Peter Stark graduate program, at the University of Southern California, that today everything is in the "fast lane" with little time for preparation. "If an actor has three interviews in one day, perhaps he or she should ask the agent to postpone one of them. And don't be afraid to get as much information as you need. This is your time, and you need to be as prepared as you can to be the best you can." When it comes to casting, Pam Dixon relies on instinct. "That's what makes each of us different from one another: taste and instinct. If you line up five of the top casting directors and have one actor audition, you'll probably get five different opinions."

Susan Edelman

BUCK/EDELMAN CASTING

Partner: Mary V. Buck
4045 Radford Ave., Suite B
Studio City, CA 91604
(818) 506-7328

Susan Edelman started out as an assistant for several prominent casting directors in Los Angeles before going independent and teaming up with Mary Buck. As a matter of fact, one of those with whom she assisted, early on, was Buck, who was head of casting for Paramount Television when Edelman applied for a job with the specific understanding that she would be allowed to cast her own show. "A year later," she recalls, "I was given the opportunity to cast *Mork and Mindy* in its last year, when Jonathan Winters was in it. That's when I became a full-fledged casting director."

The year was 1981. The following season Mary Buck left Paramount to open her own company and asked Edelman to be her associate. "I worked with her about a year when I was offered a job at CBS as a director of casting. I said to Mary I'd be leaving unless she wanted to partner with me, which she agreed to immediately. We teamed up in 1984, and it's been well over thirteen years." She laughs, "That's longer than my relationship with my husband!"

One of the things Edelman feels has changed in her profession is the casting director's relationship with the agent. "When I was just starting out at Paramount, the agents all made trips to the studios and submitted their clients in person. You had a real hands-on experience. Today, people strive to do it all through the computer." But the bottom line, she believes, is that "we're still looking for that magical casting that excites people, that's creative: casting that enhances a role, that breathes life into a role in a way no one else would have thought of, that contributes to making a show stand out. For instance, when I did the pilot for *Party of Five*, the actors were virtual unknowns, and today,

CREDITS INCLUDE:
Beast
A Father For Charlie
Party of Five Pilot
Melrose Place Pilot
Killing in a Small Town
The Wonder Years

Neve Campbell is on the cover of *Rolling Stone*." Also, keeping one-self open to new ideas has always been important to Edelman, even when those ideas come from the "mouths of babes." "We were working on this one project and had trouble casting one of the young roles. We had rented a tape of a film called *The Boy Who Could Fly,* that my ten-year-old stepson Josh loved. He watched it over and over again. He kept wanting me to watch a scene in which the lead character's younger brother gets his revenge on a bunch of bullies. I finally came in to see it, and there was a little boy named Fred Savage." Fred's agent, Iris Burton, agreed to send the script to the Savages in Chicago. They had no interest in moving to Los Angeles, but apparently after reading the *Wonder Years* pilot, they were hooked.

Television, says Edelman, is a tough nut to crack for actors. "Particularly pilots. It's a miracle that anybody gets cast, because you have to survive a reading with us, a reading with the producers, then approval by the studio, the director, and the network. There can be as much pressure in film, depending on the stakes. The greater the stakes, the greater the number of people involved in the decision. There's tremendous pressure all around." That, of course, doesn't mean Edelman and Buck play only a minor part in the process. "One of the strengths of our company is the way we behave. I think one reason we're hired is that we're passionate, very opinionated, and never shy about expressing our opinions. Occasionally it gets us in trouble, but primarily it's beneficial."

What impresses them most is professionalism on the part of the actor. "Actors must be prepared. They have to understand the project, know their sides, and show they've really worked on them. And then there's that something you can't quite explain—that magical something. If I could pinpoint it, I could bottle it and retire."

Edelman understands the actor's frustration with all the competition in Hollywood. "This town is filled with the prettiest girls and the most handsome boys in America, but I believe an actor should pursue his art not because he was the cutest in his hometown play but because he has a passion and deep belief in it." She admits she can spot artists when they walk through the door. "They have something very special, and they bring a depth to the audition that you can quickly see when you've interviewed two hundred people for the same role."

Working on *Significant Others,* for Fox, she remarks, "We'll read a thousand actors for a pilot, or more! For this project, where we're looking for a group of unknown twenty-five-year-olds, we've gone through all the actors in town. We've contacted all the regional theaters to send us information. We have someone in New York keeping their eyes open, and I'm about to hire some casting directors in Toronto and Vancouver to help out."

The most frustrating part of casting, to Edelman, is the time factor. "It's difficult when they want you to cast something in a hour or two, and you never feel like you've been able to explore all the possibilities or be as creative as you'd like. But I love the process. Casting, to me, is incredibly important."

And one of the things she hopes actors understand is that just because you don't get the role you're reading for doesn't mean you won't be brought back for something else. "I know exactly what they're looking for in each role, and maybe you don't have the physical characteristics they need. It doesn't mean you didn't do a wonderful job, or that I didn't think you'd be right for a myriad other roles. I will remember you."

Sylvia Fay

71 Park Ave.
New York, NY 10016
(212) 889-2626
FAX (212) 684-5939

Sylvia Fay never works alone. Because of the nature of her casting jobs, she works closely with her staff and always teams up with colleagues. She enjoys her collaborations with Juliet Taylor, Lynn Kressel, Ellen Lewis and many others. While they cast the primary speaking roles, she casts the one-liners and extras. On some occasions, if the casting director needs assistance, she'll be asked to pitch in on other roles or give an actor who isn't right for a bigger role in a particular feature an assignment as an extra.

Fay finds much of her talent through open calls, which she holds several times a year. She'll see more than fifteen hundred people at a single session. "I have a very good memory," she tells actors. "I give them all my wonderful speech, and then my assistants interview them and collect their photos and résumés. One girl asked how I'd know if she could act. I told her if she were right for something, I'd be calling her. She asked if I actually read the résumés. I said, 'Certainly. That's how I cast.'"

The biggest difference between casting principals and extras is in the quantity of people Fay has to deal with. "We do it in bulk," she explains. "I may need twenty well-dressed people for a party scene, or a hundred. I try to get as close to the actual situation as possible. If you were a cop, I'd use you as a cop. I try to get as much realism for a director as possible." Of course, she adds, she'll also consider an actor for other characters, but if he or she has a skill, she'll put it to good use.

When she's casting bit parts, she'll pre-screen the actors and then send them to the director for what she calls a "look-see." If the director is interested, he or she will read them or sometimes meet them on the set if the film is in the middle of shooting. Because of the limited size of the part, an actor will rarely get more than a

CREDITS INCLUDE:
Meet Joe Black
In and Out
Donnie Brasco
For Richer or Poorer
Private Parts
Law & Order

couple of hours, if that, to look over the sides. They're cold readings with either Fay or one of her assistants, and she will bring in only a select few for each part. Since she does the selecting, she has no need for the use of videotape at auditions, and she does no call-backs. It's a simple one-step process.

"I have certain cards I print up for all the actors I meet at open calls," she explains. "They tell me everything I need to know: whether they ride a bicycle, roller skate, play the piano, or use a stethoscope. The actors fill out these cards, listing all their capabili-ties. I go through these cards when I'm casting a particular project and bring in those I feel are best suited for the role." And she stress-es that if an actor puts down on the card that he or she rides a bike, it had better be something that person has done recently, not fifteen years ago as a kid.

Years of theatrical training isn't as important to Fay as arriving on the set on time, being alert, and paying attention to what the assistant director and director are saying. In general, studying may not necessarily impress Fay, but acting lessons are a help to the actor, and studying with a good coach will catch her attention on the résumé.

Fay is always looking for new talent at open calls, on the street, or even in restaurants. "It's a habit of mine when I'm walking down the street or having dinner in a cafe. My eyes are always open." She keeps a sharp lookout at the theater, and at workshops and show-cases, which she frequently attends. If someone she spots is really special, she'll often turn him or her over to a principal casting direc-tor. She definitely wants to see her discoveries succeed. "I have a great eye," she concedes. "And I enjoy it. It's a big job dealing with SAG and with so many personalities. But I must say, I've made a big change in extras casting. I want my people to get the best atten-tion on the set, to have the best places to dress and to wait. It's very important to them and to me."

In Warwick, Rhode Island, casting five hundred actors for three weeks of nighttime shoots on *Meet Joe Black.* (with Anthony Hop-kins and Brad Pitt), she observes: "These people from a small town—there's an amazing number of talented people. We just had a talent show, and you wouldn't believe how professionally many of them performed." They're all politicking for their SAG cards, she laughed, but she's delighted with the enthusiasm, especially since these local actors are working from 6 P.M. to 6 A.M. night after night.

Sylvia Fay has seen too many actors make the leap from bit play-ers to feature performers to shrug anyone off as a nonentity. She remembers when Danny Aiello and his sons came to her for work just to keep busy, and now they're turning offers down. "Danny had the humility and the warmth. He knew what he wanted. He knew it was a business. Don't think for a minute that acting isn't just like being successful in running a restaurant or boutique. They're exactly the same. It's the attention you give that business that will determine your eventual success."

Mike Fenton

MIKE FENTON & ASSOCIATES

Associate: Allison Cowitt
14724 Ventura Blvd. #510
Sherman Oaks, CA 91403
(818) 501-0177
FAX (818) 501-0188

Mike Fenton, a casting director for more than thirty years, has had his own business since 1971. He is responsible for casting many films and, as a consultant, has helped various European producers with casting and with recruiting directors and other primary production personnel.

Starting out as a casting director for Paramount Pictures in the 1960s, Fenton joined forces with Fred Roos in 1971. When Roos was hired by Francis Ford Coppola as his producer, Fenton teamed with another partner, Jane Feinberg, who retired in '87. Since then it has been Mike Fenton & Associates, a team reponsible for casting some of the biggest films of the last decade, including *Back to the Future, Dante's Peak,* and *Total Recall.*

Fenton really knows actors and what they go through pursuing a career in the business. In his opinion, the majority of actors who succeed are people who have been educated. "I don't think there's much place in this business for people who've not at least studied the classics," he postulates. "There are always actors who drop in out of the sky and get a pilot though they've done nothing before, and they can possibly have a career for a while, but when the chips are down and they're asked to walk onto a Broadway stage, I think their lack of training shows."

Fenton has a knack for selecting potential stars. He was responsible for giving Kevin Costner the opportunity to read when director Kevin Reynolds was casting *Fandango.* Fenton was not casting the project but was consulting on the film and knew they were having dif-

CREDITS INCLUDE:
Lost in Space
Dante's Peak
Honeymoon in Vegas
Aliens
Back to the Future

47

ficulty finding their leading man. A friend of his at William Morris Agency happened to show him a videotape of Kevin Costner in a one-minute TV commercial for a computer product. Fenton was impressed and asked if he could show it to Reynolds. Reynolds was as impressed as Fenton, and Costner got his big break. "Who knows what it is these stars have?" he wonders. "You certainly can't bottle it. It's just charisma—an intelligence."

Fenton doesn't read actors. "I can't. I don't have the time. It's up to the agents to make us really aware of actors with whom we should become familiar." But even though he doesn't read actors, he definitely likes to meet them. "If one of the agents with whom we work closely calls and says: 'I have an actress just in from Broadway, and she's a hit,' I meet her." He prefers leaving the reading to the director. "That's what they get paid for. If an agent calls me and says this individual starred in a particular project, far be it for me to pass judgment on that individual."

Work connotes professionalism in Fenton's estimation. "On a given day, any actor can be wonderful, any actor can be terrible. Some actors can't read well. Should that preclude their being in a motion picture? Not in my opinion." Unlike most casting directors, Fenton believes those in his profession insult actors by making them read. "Agents build careers," he explains. "All a casting director can do is recommend somebody."

Fenton also avoids going out in search of an actor. "There are thousands of character actors. If we can't find one among the people with whom we have worked, then we don't know this business." He does, however, try to attend films and theater as much as possible so that when an agent asks if he's seen his client, he can respond intelligently. As for the actors' guides and directories, he only uses them as a refresher to see who's out there.

Fenton strays from the norm in his use of videotape when a director is out of town. He'll use video and film when a lead character is under consideration. He cites the casting of *White Fang*: "Randall Kleiser and I put people on tape; then film testing was done, and from that the decision was made." Because it's a costly process, he admits this procedure isn't used unless the actor is a major contender. "It takes a sizable budget to justify a screen test, but when you're looking for the young lead in a film, you'd be well served to do it."

Sensitive to actors, Fenton tries not to schedule readings for the same part at the same time. This consideration, however, is sometimes difficult to achieve. "When we're pressed for time, it's impossible. But actors know that when they're reading for a part, they're in competition for the job."

Mike Fenton's primary advice to actors: "Remember that if you're called in for a meeting with a director, it's because we believe that you have the necessary skills to do the job. We are the actor's friend; not the actor's adversary."

Howard Feuer

c/o Casting Society of America
311 W. 43rd St. #700
New York, NY 10036
(212) 333-4552

When Howard Feuer was a student at Emerson College, he wanted to be an actor, but as soon as he began working for a producer and watching hundreds of actors audition, he realized acting wasn't for him. "I just didn't have the drive, let alone the ability," he admits. It's not that he didn't give it a shot. He landed a number of small parts, but he felt he wasn't really getting anywhere. It was then that director Gilbert Cates gave Feuer the chance to help him cast one of his plays. "I didn't know what the hell I was doing. How could I?—I'd never done it. But I got through it." From there, he moved on to an apprenticeship with an established casting agency.

"The most difficult part of being a casting director," he explains, "is having to work with directors you may not see eye to eye with." This happened to him on *Stella*, a Bette Midler vehicle. Feuer was doing another project at the time, for Disney, and he felt a little short-changed when the schedule for the Disney film was altered, interfering with his new assignment. Instead of understanding his dilemma, the director apparently tried to get Feuer fired from Disney. But Disney wouldn't let him out of his contract. "The main problem was, the director was indecisive. He didn't like the actors. He couldn't make up his mind. Instead of firing me, he was abusive and immature. When I'd bring key actors to his attention, he simply picked people he knew." Feuer realizes now he should have simply quit. "I always had the philosophy that, if you're a professional, you'll get through it, but I've changed my mind. If someone treats you badly, and they're not smart enough to fire you, you should be smart enough to call it quits."

Fortunately, those situations don't happen very often; in fact, Feuer's so much in

CREDITS INCLUDE:
The Truman Show
Beloved
That Thing You Do
Philadelphia
Silence of the Lambs

demand, he can pick and choose for whom he works from the highest echelon of filmmakers. He has solid working relationships with Alan Parker, Peter Yates, Peter Weir, and Norman Jewison. Working with Jewison on *Moonstruck*, for instance, was especially satisfying; Feuer was allowed a great deal of flexibility in the casting. "I thought of Olympia Dukakis," he fondly recalls. "She was a first-rate stage actress at the time. We all knew her in New York. When I met with Jewison, he expressed dismay at the fact they didn't have enough money to hire Anne Bancroft or Maureen Stapleton for the part, and I thought of Olympia immediately. In fact, I was able to use all these New York character actors I'd known for years." The film, incidentally, was cast in just three and a half weeks, and Dukakis won an Academy Award for her performance.

Feuer experienced a similar feeling of accomplishment upon completion of *That Thing You Do* for first-time director Tom Hanks. "Everyone came out of the woodwork to be seen for Tom's film, and he loved every single actor I brought in." Most had little, if any, experience—including Tom Everett Scott, who played the lead, and Charlize Theron, who was twenty at the time. "When Charlize walked out the door, Tom said to me, 'She's going to be a star!' She was so good we had her read for two of the female parts. She could have played either one. She's unusually interesting, touching, and funny." Apparently, others in the business agreed. She immediately went on to star in *Mighty Joe Young*.

Feuer has helped a great many actors with their careers. "I was the first to use Meg Ryan in a feature film," he relates with much pride. "She was a student at NYU, and I was doing the East Coast casting for *Rich and Famous*. We were looking for someone to play Candace Bergen's daughter, and Meg was perfect." And when he cast *Married to the Mob*, he campaigned heartily for Alec Baldwin as Michelle Pfeiffer's husband, despite the director's preliminary reluctance to use this "newcomer."

Despite his ability, Feuer says he would never want a director to leave the casting entirely to him. "Even the tiniest role should be seen by the director. I wouldn't be comfortable with it. A terrific filmmaker has a very specific vision. Even if it means putting an actor on tape and getting it to the director, I like him or her to say, 'Yes, this is what I want.'"

Since Feuer has a great deal of acting training, he wouldn't dream of hiring anyone else to read with actors at auditions. In rare instances, however, a director will insist on reading. One such director is Alan Parker. "Alan likes to read with actors in private.

I'll bring an actor to him, and he'll insist on being alone with that actor. He then videotapes the reading, so eventually I'll get to see the audition, but I'm not allowed to sit in on it. He'll hold the camera and tape while he reads the scene. I think it's because he wants the most intimate feeling he can get with the least amount of pressure on the actor to perform."

Any actor who won't read for a director gets a demerit in Feuer's book. "In New York, most actors have no qualms about reading for a director, no matter how successful they are. Actors there are used to having to hustle for a part. In California, however, actors are often pampered. They never have to do it, and so they don't. They have superlative agents who are very good at protecting them." So he was very impressed when Jeff Bridges agreed to read for director Terry Gilliam on *The Fisher King*. "The character, on paper, reads like a very aggressive New Yorker, so we thought in more ethnic terms. That didn't seem right, so we sought out Bruce Willis or Michael Keaton. They weren't available. Then we thought of a middle-American male, to make it more of a Prince Charming fairy tale, and I immediately suggested Jeff." Gilliam's problem was that he hadn't worked with American actors very much, and with Bridges he felt he needed a little more confirmation. "Obligingly, Jeff agreed to read for the part, since he really wanted it. It was so different from what he'd ever done." Even successful actors may have to please the powers that be.

It's common to find Feuer jetting between New York and Los Angeles. Many of his projects are bicoastal, and instead of splitting the work with another casting director, Feuer prefers to endure the jet lag and do the job himself. That's one of the reasons he isn't as accessible to newcomers as many other casting directors. He just doesn't have the time. He finds himself relying on agents he trusts and on referrals from friends and colleagues. Working on several films a year, he realizes the day may come when he has to face the dreaded job burnout. But so far, he doesn't mind putting up with the long hours and tedious cross-country hops.

Don't be surprised, however, if you soon see Howard Feuer's name featured more prominently in the credits. He's admittedly on the lookout for a good property to produce.

Alan Filderman

Partner: Michelle Ortlip
630 Ninth Ave., Suite 800
New York, NY 10036
(212) 459-9462

Alan Filderman understands actors. He, at one time, wanted to be an actor himself. "That's why I moved to New York," he says, where he supported himself by working in restaurants, as so many unemployed actors have done and continue to do. Tired of waiting tables but intent on staying in the business in some capacity, Filderman ventured into theatrical management. "That's how I learned the business," he explains. "I found out what an agent, casting director, and manager do. And, of all the professions, I found casting to be the most interesting. I was on the phone all the time with casting directors, and I just let it be known that I was available."

Then one day it happened. Mary Colquhoun, a prominent casting director in New York, needed an assistant. That was about ten years ago. Today Filderman is a respected casting director in his own right.

Although he does cast Broadway, off-Broadway, and film, he specializes in regional theater. Casting in this field differs somewhat: "Casting for regional theater happens faster," he explains. "The producers come in from out of town and usually have three or four days to find their actors. It's a sped-up process, and your choices are slimmer because not every actor wants to do regional theater"— which displeases him. "Actors simply don't want to leave town, if they can help it. We've reached the point where they want to stay in New York or Los Angeles so they're available to audition for film and TV." And it's not so much the actors as their agents and managers who make that decision. "Agents would rather have their clients unemployed and available to audition for film and TV than working in the theater. It's become an epidemic. Actors often feel they have to listen to

CREDITS INCLUDE:
Master Class Broadway/Touring
Once on This Island Broadway/Touring
Three Tall Women Off-Broadway/Touring
Broadway Damage Feature

53

their agents and turn down great theater, just so they can be available for a pilot."

When an actor comes along willing to do regional theater, Filderman is thrilled. "You find actors who are smart enough to know they should do regional theater—real actors intent on working at their craft for at least two or three years before they worry about television and film. You also find actors who are tired of L.A. and dying to get back to the stage. And you find actors who care more about stage than the other media."

Regional theater, says Filderman, is not a dead-end job. There have been a number of actors who've been "discovered" out of town. "There's an actor named Neil Maffin," he cites, who co-stars opposite Antonio Banderas in the Michael Crichton film *Eaters of the Dead*. He's someone I cast in at least five regional plays. I didn't cast the Crichton film, but that's where Maffin made his mark. And there are a number of films which I've cast with actors who've been devoted to regional theater over the years. I know the true trained actors, and when I do cast film, I definitely lean toward those who've done regional theater."

When Filderman is casting a play or film, his first step is to read the script. His second is to talk to the director. "I find out his or her views on the various roles. I write up a breakdown and submit it to Breakdown Services, which sends it out to agents. Once I get submissions, I go through them and decide who I think should come in to audition. I add the actors I know to the lists, and then we proceed with auditions." The number of actors per role depends on the medium. For an off-Broadway play, he may bring in twenty or thirty actors per character, whereas if he's casting a regional production for a shorter run, he may call in ten. And he's constantly seeing new actors as replacements in long-running shows.

Each show has its own challenge. "When I'm casting a classic play, I need actors who are trained and skilled in classical theater, who are comfortable with the language and stage movement. For contemporary theater, I need actors who are very connected to themselves with vibrant personalities and charisma. For musicals, obviously, they have to sing and dance. There are very different skills required for every type of theater." Training is vital. "I work with a lot of directors who aren't even interested in seeing an actor unless they're out of a training program. It doesn't have to be NYU or Yale, but unless you're drop-dead gorgeous or have a lot of charm, you need some sort of formal training if you want attention."

What annoys Filderman are those actors who walk into auditions with an Irving Berlin song when the call is for contemporary Broadway. "It's part of the preparation. If I say a certain type of song is required, that's what I expect. If it's picking up the sides the day before or being on time, that's what's required." He also frowns on actors crashing auditions. "Only come in if you have an appointment," he warns. "Sometimes an actor will hear about an audition from a friend. I've never hired anyone who tries to sneak in. They have to be on the list."

It's important for actors to attend Equity Principal Auditions, according to Filderman. "When I was casting *Once on This Island,* for Broadway, two people who came in on the EPA auditions wound up getting cast, and one, La Chanze, who went on to *Ragtime,* got nominated for a Tony."

A couple of times a year Filderman tries to do generals, where he'll meet new actors who were submissions or referred to him by agents and friends. He usually asks actors to prepare a pair of two-minute monologues: one contemporary and one classical. "It's better that they're not original works, because I find myself judging the playwriting and trying to figure out what they're talking about. It's much better to go with established material." An actor may think it bores casting directors to hear the same material over and over again, and for some that's true, but it's not the case with Filderman. "It really comes down to how well the actor performs it. An actor can do the most original and interesting piece in the world, but if it isn't done well, we remember the piece, not the actor. You can come in and sing 'Tomorrow,' from *Annie,* but if you sing it better than anyone else who's sung it, it works."

Leonard Finger

LEONARD FINGER CASTING

1501 Broadway #1511
New York, NY 10036
(212) 944-8611
FAX (212) 997-0135

If you enjoy scary movies and TV shows, then the name Leonard Finger may be familiar. If the piece is spooky, Finger's name could very well be in the closing credits. He's cast *Tales from the Darkside* and *Monsters,* and is the New York contact for *Goosebumps.* On the big screen, he's done a couple of Stephen King projects, which has contributed to his title within the casting community, "the King of Horror."

"The business is nothing but associations," he advises, "and it just so happened that I had clients who were working in the horror field. I simply kept doing it and kept getting referrals." Does it bother him that he's been "type-cast?" Not at all. "The one thing about it is that it gives me the opportunity to discover people and provide work for new actors, and that's enjoyable."

Some people might think that horror films require exotic or unusual-looking actors, but Finger is seeking exactly the same thing other casting directors are searching for: people with great comic timing and wonderful dramatic ability. As far as their looks are concerned, he wants pretty faces and interesting character types, just as his colleagues do. He also casts not-so-scary movies: He worked on *Mr. Holland's Opus, Pinocchio,* and *Invasion of Privacy,* and he's cast three films for Paul Morrissey.

There are special skills, however, for which he's always on the lookout. When Finger is scanning a résumé he'll take note of an actor who can speak an unusual language or perform an unusual feat such as rolling his eyes in separate directions or wiggling his ears. He also has a file of impersonators and actors who are good at creating interesting sound

CREDITS INCLUDE:
The Night Flier
Thinner
Mr. Holland's Opus
Goosebumps NY Casting
Monsters
Tales from the Darkside

effects. Finger enjoys the flexibility he has with his genre. He can almost always cast against type and create fascinating characters. When he was doing *Tales from the Darkside* one season, he happened to meet an East Asian actor who had a beautiful Kensington accent. "It had a marvelous sort of urbane decadence to it that I thought was really great. I'd brought him in for another project, but I thought what a wonderful twist to cast him as a vampire on *Darkside*."

Finger is not afraid to take chances. "I think most people want somebody else to take the first chance. They want to know that somebody else hired an actor, and that the actor didn't get drunk or disappear. To me, if it weren't for the enjoyment of discovery, I'd be doing something else. The fulfilling part of this is that sense of constantly finding talent, nurturing it, and allowing it to be rewarded. That's what I like most about casting. If I stop taking chances, I might as well get out of the business and open up a store or something."

Finger sees his role in casting as someone who provides the intervention of reality. He feels that many actors are blind when it comes to seeing who they really are. "When you ask actors how they felt about an audition, they'll say, 'I felt really good about it.' That's absolutely ridiculous—it's not what the actor feels that matters; it's what the audience, the people watching the actor perform feel. It's about being evocative, not self-congratulatory." If an actor is going to judge a performance, he believes it should always be through the responses of others. "What I'm saying is almost in direct conflict with a sanctioned narcissism among acting teachers, a kind of acting I really think is destructive."

As a matter of fact, Finger is not a proponent of acting classes. Although he admires a well-trained actor, he thinks many young actors are wasting their money on the majority of classes that are out there. "To me, the best thing you can buy is a directory of all the people working in the industry—learn the vocabulary of names—because at this point, it's all associations. Training is not nearly as important so long as you can deliver the lines. If you have real ability, it will be cultivated. If someone really has talent, teachers will come to that person, whether he or she has money or not. I've seen that happen time and time again."

He also suggests that actors pay attention to what's on TV, in films, and on stage. "See who is like you, who is getting cast, who's doing the casting, and what the shows are about. Know what you're selling," he advises, "and learn to market it."

He also advises learning what doesn't work in your favor. For instance, when you're being interviewed by a casting director, focus on your attributes rather than your liabilities. "One actor who came in for a prescreening told me how much he wanted meaningful parts, but that he kept getting in trouble with directors for arguing with them about the interpretation of a character. He was, in essence, telling me he was a risk to hire. It wouldn't be a service to my director to hire someone like that. He was revealing himself beyond what I wanted to know." An important lesson to actors: This is not psychoanalysis. This is a job. Keep it professional and on target.

Finger gets a sense of an actor in the first thirty seconds of a meeting. "I also get a sense of whether actors have ability in the first minute and a half." Therefore, he keeps his auditions short and to the point. "I get the actors to come in, treat them nicely, and don't engage in too much chit-chat, because all that does is heighten their anxiety. I just want them in and out." During a reading, Finger expects an actor to be in character, but before the reading he's looking to see the person behind the mask. He discourages costumes or props. "An actor should convey the character by acting, not with superficial or external things."

Finger is a student of classic theater. He loves plays set in the nineteenth and early twentieth centuries, and he also loves finding actors from the past. "I think we're a society of fashions, and actors are a fashion, too, with people having a moment of popularity and then falling from view. I like to rediscover them." He did just that with one actress in particular, who was the original Effie in *You Can't Take It with You* on Broadway. He cast Paula Truman in one of his TV series, and she's been busy ever since. Other stars with more familiar names, whose careers were on the slide but who've reemerged thanks to Finger, include Abe Vigoda, Darren McGavin, Debbie Harry, and Carol Lynley.

He's also made some promising discoveries on the streets of New York. When he was casting *Forty-Deuce* for Paul Morrissey, they found Rodney Harvey literally on the street. "We started talking to this kid and brought him up to my office. We found out he was interested in acting, talked to his mother, and got her permission to put him in the film." From there, Harvey got a recurring role on the series, *The Outsiders*.

While discovering untrained actors may be fun and challenging, Finger gets most of his actors from the stage—"people with training and a real awareness of training. I can't begin to tell you how many theater people I've gotten into SAG." He considers himself a businessman first, and an artist second. "To me, we are accomplices of the director. We are serving out someone else's vision, and I look at it most definitely as a business." And that's exactly how he sees acting. "There are a few artists who manage to struggle through and survive, but there's very little art in what's done today. There are a lot of actors I tremendously respect, but very few are artists."

Should an actor give himself a time limit in which to succeed? "Of course," says Finger. "There's an old Talmudic saying: When three men say you're drunk, lie down." He thinks that actors have to have a cutoff point when they realize they're not getting what they want out of it. "The first and foremost thing is to enjoy one's life, to be functioning, and if that's not happening, it's time to move on to something else."

Jerold Franks

JEROLD FRANKS & ASSOCIATES

c/o Casting Society of America
606 N. Larchmont Blvd. #4B
Los Angeles, CA 90004
(213) 463-1925
FAX (213) 851-3681

Jerold Franks is a writer as well as a veteran casting director. His book *So You Want to Be an Actor? Act Like One*, explains his philosophy of casting and exactly what actors should avoid when trying to get their careers in gear. It's an invaluable resource. Franks has a genuine respect for actors and paints an optimistic picture for their future.

"Actors have a much better shot today, because instead of going just for the Ken and Barbie look, we're going for all kinds of faces—real, interesting, everyday faces." He feels that's what contributed to the success of *Baghdad Cafe*, for which he won the coveted Casting Society of America's Artios Award for feature casting. "Every face in that picture was a real face," he explained. Even Jack Palance was cast in a role originally written for an artistic, romantic type. "The producer and director couldn't visualize him at all, because he usually plays more menacing roles. But we fought and fought and finally got the producer to have lunch with Jack. The minute they met, he signed him right on the spot!" That film also helped resurrect Palance's career.

Franks really enjoys trying to bring in actors who may not be the obvious first choice. When he was doing an episodic TV show, he recalls having to cast the part of a pimp who was written as a Mafia type. "I changed it to a black actor who looked like an attorney. Wardrobe even dressed him like an attorney, and it worked much better, because it was a surprise element at the end of the script." That is one of the things Franks finds most challenging about casting. "There's nothing more exciting

CREDITS INCLUDE:
The Parsley Garden
Baghdad Cafe
Fame Episodic
Matters of the Heart
The Unsinkable Molly Brown
Touring

than when an actor walks in and you can tell by instinct that there's something there. That's what casting is all about, always looking for the interesting."

He says he found that quality in Mickey Rourke when he was casting a project for Columbia back in 1980. "His agent brought him in. He had never done anything in his life except theater; he didn't even have a union card. But the minute he walked in, there was a sense of incredible energy. I thought he was perfect for the role, so I took him to the producer and director the next day. And while the reading was wonderful, they didn't feel that physically he was the right type. They went, instead, with Robert Ricardo, simply because of his coloring." It was shortly after that episode that Rourke made a hit in his first feature, *Body Heat*.

Franks prides himself on his ability to look beyond the facade to the inner actor. He knew there were the makings of a star when he first auditioned Emma Samms, the English actress. He introduced her to producer Gloria Monty, who was looking for one of the regulars on *General Hospital* and was quite impressed with her reading. She did feel, however, that Emma was too young for the part. Franks felt differently and suggested that with makeup and a new hairdo she could fit the role to a tee. "Gloria said, 'If you feel that strongly, bring her back,' and sure enough, we brought her back dressed older, and they flipped over her!"

Franks feels just as adamant about casting pilots. "That's why casting directors see so many people for pilots, because someone is the 'perfect' person. Look at any given hit, and you can't think of anybody who would have been in that role who could have done any better."

His desire for precision has led Franks to cast a variety of disabled actors in roles that do and do not call for disabled characters. He cast James Stacey in the role of a Vietnam vet, opposite Jane Seymour, in *A Matter of Trust*. Stacey, a star in the 1960s, unfortunately lost two limbs in a motorcycle accident, but thanks to casting directors like Franks, he has had an opportunity to continue his career. Another example was the casting of *Superior Court*. "There was a wonderful actress who happens to be blind, and I brought her in to read for a character seated in a witness chair. The reading was so good, the director never knew until the end of the day that she was blind. When he expressed his concern, I explained that she didn't even have to walk into the room. And if you look at the tape of the show, you'd never know. The point is," he adds, "she was a very competent actress. It's the same thing as hiring someone in a wheelchair who sits behind a desk. What's the difference if he can't stand up?"

When Franks, who spent a year as an agent at Metropolitan Talent, meets actors, he prefers a general interview to a cold reading. "I'd rather know who they are, and what their goals are, and if they're newcomers just starting out." He also never asks an actor to read at generals. "I don't believe in monologues. Somebody could study a monologue for three years—and that's all they know. It's not going to show me anything." He prefers reading someone for an appropriate role, and that's what he does when he calls an actor back for an audition.

At the audition, Franks discourages actors from smoking. "Even if the casting director smokes, it's inappropriate for the actor to." The other thing he cautions actors about is their dress. "I treat this business like a profession because it is, and I don't think actors should arrive in shorts and a T-shirt. They don't need to go out and buy a new wardrobe. They do need to be clean and neat."

Actors should also avoid trying to impress a casting director. "It shows a lot of insecurity when someone comes in and pretends to be something he's not. The most important thing in a general interview is being who you are. That's what I'm looking for. I want to see who the person is, rather than the actor. Also, I don't like a cocky attitude."

Franks tries to impart to actors that they're perfect the way they are, and there's no need to look around the reception area to see who the competition is. "Actors cannot sit and compare. It's a waste of energy, and they need to put that energy into themselves and the role—period. That's it!"

Jan Glaser

CONCORDE-NEW HORIZONS CORP.

Associate: Jerry Whitworth
1600 San Vicente Blvd.
Los Angeles, CA 90049
(310) 820-6733
FAX (310) 207-6816

One of the tools that casting directors seldom utilize but which frequently comes in handy for Jan Glaser is videotape. As Vice President of Talent for Roger Corman's film company, Glaser is always busy putting actors on tape. "The directors need to see the choices, especially if they're out of town. With tape, you can always refer to the videos when a producer or director doesn't remember an actor I'm suggesting for a project. It provides a good reference."

Glaser loves her work. She usually casts two or three cable TV or direct-to-video movies each month. Many are filmed at the Corman facility in Ireland. She is always looking for new talent, which she finds through agents—particularly agents with whom she's had success—and submissions. Glaser also relies heavily on the *Academy Players Directory*, thumbing through it to find faces that are right for specific parts. While SAG actors are her first choice, she'll consider anyone who may be right for the role.

At the audition, Glaser expects an actor to stick to the script—no improvising. "A lot of our writers are very sensitive," she explains. "They don't like their words played around with." She is also opposed to actors memorizing lines, preferring that they have the sides in their hands.

Intelligent questions from an actor are appreciated, and Glaser will in turn ask actors about themselves and what else they do with their time besides acting. "I'm interested in knowing if they've taken a cooking class or gone scuba diving. I may need someone with those skills down the line, and it'll stick with me."

What really catches Glaser's attention is a sense of humor. That's one of the things

CREDITS INCLUDE:
Overdrive
Pay Back
Alien Avengers 1 & 2
Scene of the Crime

she first noticed about Kirstie Alley, whom she met early on in her career. "There was just something really special about her; a natural, funny quality." It's not beauty that's important to Glaser; it's more of an offbeat quality that captivates her.

What she doesn't like are gum chewing and cigarette smoking, even if they might be appropriate for a character. "It's just annoying to watch," she imparts. She also doesn't like anyone in her office rearranging her desk or asking to borrow a stapler. "I can't tell you how often people ask to borrow a pen to write down their latest credits. Do that in the waiting area or at home." And don't harass her assistant, even if you've been waiting a long time. She realizes it's often frustrating to be kept waiting, but she insists she does the best she can under the circumstances, and that it certainly isn't her assistant's fault.

Glaser isn't fond of people coming up to her in social situations asking for work, although it did pay off for her golf pro. He had always wanted to act. "When I was taking lessons he'd tell me the things he'd done, and one day I brought him in to read for the role of the monster in *Watchers Four.* Talk about prepared! He told me how he'd gotten into character: He went to the zoo. He vacuumed in character. I told the director, who was impressed that he'd taken the role so seriously. He got the job." She smiles. "I don't think I take golf as seriously as he takes acting!"

Another tip for actors: Make sure your name appears on the front of your headshots as well as on your résumé, and keep your pictures up to date in the *Academy Players Directory.* Glaser discourages phone calls asking for her address or directions to her office. She prefers that you ask your agent for that information or check a directory. If you need to inform her that you're appearing in a play, send her a flyer instead of calling. Postcards with a photo are appropriate reminders of an actor's whereabouts and a way to keep in touch. And while it may not be quite orthodox, Glaser admits she has an awfully sweet tooth and occasionally succumbs to a favorite dessert.

Laura Gleason

LAURA GLEASON CASTING

15030 Ventura Blvd. #747
Sherman Oaks, CA 91403
(818) 906-9767

I t's not uncommon for a casting director to start his or her career as an actor. Such was the case with Laura Gleason. "I'd always acted from the time I was a child and had attended Northwestern University as a theater major. I graduated from UCLA in Theater Arts and attended the Neighborhood Playhouse, in New York, and American Conservatory Theater, in San Francisco." But, she says, "I got very frustrated with the lack of work as I got older. All of a sudden it seemed to dry up."

That's when her husband suggested she stretch herself artistically and find another outlet for her talent. "I'd known Leslie Moonves when he was working in New York for a theater production company. He suggested I check out an opening at the New York Shakespeare Festival, Joseph Papp's operation, so I jumped on it." It was a fruitful lead. Soon Gleason was the casting associate for Papp's Public Theater. "I basically learned about the process from all the casting directors working there. It was the best place to learn, because they were always doing five plays at once, seeing every actor in New York."

Her next move was to agenting. "It was fun, but my heart wasn't in it. I still wanted to cast and even did a little moonlighting in film and theater until a job became available at ABC." She was at the right place at the right time. "They decided they were going to do a new soap, *Loving,* and I became the casting director." She stayed in that position until the birth of her first child three years later. Parenting became her priority, and over the next several years she occasionally did casting for a friend here and there.

Fate then brought her to the West Coast, where she hoped to provide a

CREDITS INCLUDE:
High Tide
Loving
Counselor at Law Theater
Ad Wars Theater
Home Free All

more pleasant environment for her family. She returned to business full-time, had a good time working on *Counselor at Law,* with John Rubinstein—it garnered twenty-six awards including the L.A. Drama Critics Circle Award— and later cast a syndicated series called *High Tide,* starring Rick Springfield. "It's nice working in syndication, because you're trying to please the owners of the company and the producers; you're not dealing with the network. Not that network people can't be charming and knowledgeable; it just cuts out one more middle-man. So it's a little easier to cast for syndication."

Her favorite part of the casting process? "Meeting the actors," she admits. "I love to talk to them and audition them. I read with every one of them. I don't coach them unless I see there's something missing, then I'll try to direct them. I'll ask them to try it this way or that way." She recalls a British actor who just couldn't relax with the material. "He was all over the room pacing. I said 'I'm going to plant you here. Don't move. Just talk to me.' It was amazing: the energy and focus—it changed his entire audition. I brought him to the producers at that point. He didn't get the part, but it was the age factor; they really liked him and recommended him to another casting director for a different project."

It's frustrating to Gleason when she feels an actor is right for the part and the producers disagree. It happened with the now-successful Chazz Palmintieri, who was starring in an off-Broadway show at the time. "The producers just didn't want to move him to Broadway when the opportunity presented itself. The part was tailor-made for him. I was very upset, because, artistically, I thought they were making a huge mistake. He was perfect. He got huge laughs off-Broadway. For months they resisted using him for the Broadway move. I fought for him and, finally, when they told me if I mentioned his name one more time they'd fire me, I stood my ground." They conceded, but only partially. "They actually brought him in and made him audition four times. It was very cruel. He only came back because he needed the work. He was doing standup on Long Island and working at clubs as a bouncer. They ended up hiring him as an understudy. At least he got his Equity card."

Gleason continued to fight for Chazz. When she was casting a twin for one of the regulars on *Loving,* she persuaded the producers to hire the still-struggling actor. "He got about nine months of work, very steady work, which kept him afloat and made it possible for him to move to Hollywood." And that's not the only instance where Gleason has had to hold firm. Again, on *Loving*, "they were hesitant to hire Susan Keith, a wonderfully charming actress and one hundred percent right for the role. I insisted the producer meet with her and let her audition, and he did and said, 'You're right. I was wrong about her.' She was hired as a contract player and worked for many years in the role. Every time I'd meet her on the street, she'd say, 'There's the person who was responsible for my career,' and I'd say, 'Susan, *you* are responsible for your career.' But it was so sweet of her to remember, to acknowledge it. Many actors don't."

The difference between actors in New York and Los Angeles, she believes, has to do with the level of commitment. "I think actors in New York really take their craft seriously. They're in class whether they're working or not. Even models are in class. The teachers there are good, and they don't charge an arm and a leg. Out in L.A., they sometimes have a tendency to be a bit of a racket." She thinks the encouragement actors get to perform onstage in New York is also a reason they're more prepared. "That's the business of New York: the stage." She prefers to see sustained stage performances rather than showcases. "But I will do workshops," she admits. "I do ask actors to submit their pictures at least a day in advance so I can pull scenes and try to match them. I'll then read with them, one on one, and direct them. I'll even go over their résumés with them. I love to talk to actors, because you get a lot from that. It also helps me to remember them better." Though she's never actually hired actors she's met at showcases, she has brought them in to read.

When she looks at actors' résumés, it's the training and theater she first focuses on. "In L.A., it's probably listed at the bottom, but it's still what I look at first. If I recognize a play they've done or a teacher with whom they've studied, that means something to me."

"If you're right out of school, there's nothing to be ashamed of, " she adds. "Just put which school and the productions you've done there. People understand you're just getting started." You must be honest, or you could get into hot water: "I caught some credits recently that were pretty funny. An actor came in from a major hit play in which his manager said he'd played the lead. Considering that the lead was African-American and he was Caucasian, I questioned him about it, and he was really embarrassed. It was not my intent to embarrass him, but to share a bit of a laugh with him over a careless error. He said he didn't know his résumé had gone out that way. That it was his manager's doing." Your credits are your "personal legacy," and everyone wants good ones, but they have to reflect you. "If you fudge your credits," Gleason advises, "it eventually catches up with you."

Quoting a line in *The Days & Nights of Molly Dodd*, Gleason summed up: "If I have any one thing to say to an actor, I'll say what George Gaines, playing a Broadway producer in that series, said to an aspiring young actor who asked him if he had any words of advice: *Just keep at it!*"

Peter Golden

CBS ENTERTAINMENT

Associates: Michael Katcher, Lucy Cavallo, Fern Orenstein
7800 Beverly Blvd. #284
Los Angeles, CA 90036
(213) 852-2335
FAX (213) 852-2279

Peter Golden no longer does day-to-day casting, but his extensive experience in that arena provides lots of food for thought for actors. Currently the head of network talent at CBS—he supervises all CBS-network shows—Golden says he still has to be up-to-date on everyone in the acting community. "We work closely with each casting director at the network to help select our series regulars. The ultimate decision, however, is in the hands of the network executives."

Development deals are arranged through Golden's office as well as holding deals, which are his personal favorites. "I'm excited about finding actors with potential, who have a body of work or something special that interests us. We then try to put together a deal to keep them under contract. We're always looking for new talent for guest shots and series regulars."

Part of what seduced Golden into this business is what he terms his awe of actors. "There's something magical about them. I don't know how they do what they do," he admits. He does know one thing about successful actors, however, and that's their commitment to the profession. "The one thing I see about actors who come in and don't ever seem to really make it is their lack of commitment to *acting*. They'd love to be a star and make a lot of money, but when it comes to going to the Oregon Shakespeare Festival or Actors Theater of Louisville or taking classes, forget it."

Golden, who left Stephen Cannell Productions two years ago to head up talent at the network, stresses that an actor should take every audition seriously. That, he says, is the hard

CREDITS INCLUDE:
Palace Guard Pilot
Ties That Bind TV movie
The Cosby Show
Always Remember I Love You TV movie

work, and the payoff is often unrewarding, but it's a primary part of an actor's life. He recalls actor John Rubenstein telling him that he loves what he does so much that he'd perform free; his salary really goes to pay for the grueling work of the audition.

Golden says he tries to get audition material to actors at least one day before they're scheduled to come in, to give them a chance to read the script with someone else. "I want to make sure that the first time they come in, it's not the first time the words have come out of their mouths with another person in the room." As for the material utilized at an audition, Golden prefers selecting the script. He often opts for cold readings to judge whether an actor is able to listen and respond, especially at a general.

He sometimes spends a good deal of time with actors to find out about their background, but if he's short on time he'll merely read the actor, jot down a few notes, and move on. Actors seen by Golden are recruited from agents, files, and the *Academy Players Directory.* "I go through that guide constantly," he explains, "so I always recommend that people somehow get into that book." He also goes through all his mail and looks at every picture that comes in. If an actor wants to submit a new 8 x 10 or drop a line to let him know he or she is appearing in town, the timing may be perfect for getting an audition.

Even if he's pressed for time, Golden appreciates an actor asking questions about the character or material at the audition. "I wonder sometimes if people come in and don't ask questions. How could they possibly have any sense of what's going on? It makes me crazy," he adds, "when someone reads a scene and says to me later, 'By the way, is this a comedy or a drama?'"

What the actor wears is unimportant, but Golden does appreciate respect. An actor's attitude is vital, too. "I don't like seeing people who come in desperately trying to please me, because what I'm looking for are people with a very strong sense of themselves, a sense of confidence. If they're desperate, it often comes out in their performance."

If you audition for Golden, you may be one of four reading for the part—or four hundred. He may set up two or three people every fifteen minutes, and he hopes that after seeing about seventy actors, he'll hit the jackpot. "Sometimes I'm lucky and it's less, and sometimes it's a lot more." He recalls a casting session he did for *The Dick Van Dyke Show.* "We had 750 actresses read for the part. There were a lot of good readings, but no one really clicked until finally—it was the last person who came in."

Golden likes to cast minorities in roles that are not necessarily written for a specific ethnic type. His concern dates back to his days on *The Cosby Show,* when Bill Cosby asked him to bring in a mix of people simply to talk about their acting careers. "He sat down and asked them what roles they were used to playing, and they all, without exception, mentioned gang leaders and hookers and such. Cosby said, 'We're not going to do that here.' If there was a role for a pregnant woman, a doctor, any part like that, we'd instantly think, 'How can we get an Asian or Native American for this?' It was a real challenge." And that's the way Peter Golden operates today.

Jeff Greenberg

JEFF GREENBERG CASTING

Paramount Pictures
5555 Melrose Ave.
Marx Brothers Bldg. #102
Los Angeles, CA 90038
(213) 956-4886
FAX (213) 862-1368

Every week is a new challenge for me." That's the positive approach assumed by casting director Jeff Greenberg when undertaking an assignment, whether it's for Paramount, his base of operations, or for one of a number of independent projects he tackles each year.

He's always looking for new talent. "When I was working on *Cheers*," he recalls, "Sam Malone was dating a pretty girl a week; I had to be on the lookout for pretty girls." Each script requires its own set of characters. "I keep a file of interesting actors. If I like someone's background or they have an interesting look, I keep them on file."

Greenberg advises actors to do their homework before an audition. He's not impressed by someone who comes in to read and asks, "What kind of show is this?" He appreciates questions that are integral to the script, but doesn't like questions that have already been answered by the text. He suggests that actors look as much like the character for which they're auditioning as possible but without actually dressing in costume. A uniform is unnecessary if you're reading for a nurse, for instance, but a starchy white outfit would be appropriate. Attitude is much more critical to him. "I like actors to be themselves," he says. "Whatever energy they bring into the room is their own. That's very helpful."

When Greenberg sets up auditions at Paramount, actors are requested to pick up the material prior to their meeting. They either read with Greenberg or with

CREDITS INCLUDE:
A Night at the Roxbury
Father of the Bride 2
Look Who's Talking
Frasier
Cheers
Wings
My So-Called Life

one of his associates. Greenberg may provide some adjustments, or he may simply thank the actor, make some notes, and bring in the next candidate. He tries very hard not to keep actors waiting interminably and schedules his readings far enough apart in hopes of preventing that.

On the average, Greenberg puts out a breakdown for only one out of thirty parts. The fact is, he knows so many actors from his years in the business that, when it comes to adults, it's not necessary for him to recruit talent. But, he says, "If I need an Elvis imitator who can also speak Spanish, I need to put out a breakdown; I don't know enough in that category."

Greenberg also appreciates getting ideas from agents. "We're in constant communication," he acknowledges. "A lot of them call to see what's coming up, and as I talk to them about one project I might mention, 'Oh, by the way, there's another part coming up on this show on this date, if you have any ideas.'" He also uses the *Academy Players Directory,* checking it daily. "An actor is foolish," he says, "if he's not in those guides."

To Greenberg, what makes an actor right for the role is a connection with the material: "He or she enhances the material in a way that seems to originate viscerally, as opposed to coming off a page." He's impressed when an actor can create a person rather than a written character. When casting *Frasier,* for example, he was looking for the talk show host's agent. "An actress named Harriet Harris came in and read for me," he recalls. "I immediately called the producers to say I needed to show them someone right away. I brought her over in the middle of a rewrite. They flipped and hired her on the spot. She was a revelation! She had only theater experience, but she was able to come in and bring so many values to the role that weren't on the page or even how it was envisioned. It was a brilliant reading."

Kirstie Alley is another prime example. When he saw her read, he knew she was right for *Cheers.* "I knew there were very big shoes to fill when Shelley Long left the show, and it needed to be an actress of power." Alley was it, with her combination of looks, humor, and line readings. "I just knew her to be an actress unafraid to take big chances, and it was a very big chance."

Greenberg isn't as interested in an actor's film and television experience as he is in his or her regional theater background. "I want people who are fresh and have the chops to do just about everything because of their experience. Schooling is important, too, but not as much as experience."

Casting against type is often part of Greenberg's method. "If you cast too much on the nose, there are no surprises. You know what that character's going to do. It's like hiring Anthony Perkins to play the killer. There's nothing fresh about that." In hiring a minority to fill a role, Greenberg is adamant against stereotyping or quota casting. "We were looking for an emcee of an awards show on *Frasier*," he recalls, "and it was a wonderful part. We wound up using a black actor who resembled Bryant Gumbel, and it made it much more interesting, even though it hadn't been written that way."

Greenberg is also proud of his idea for the *tour de force* role of a substitute teacher on *My So-Called Life*. He brought in British actor Roger Rees, who'd never portrayed an American. "I knew Roger could do it, and he was cast."

For an actor to get noticed by Greenberg, he or she has to keep doing good work in every medium possible. "I go to the theater all the time," he says. "There's no theater I wouldn't consider attending. The only thing is, it must be a great theater experience. I don't want to see a good actor in a bad play." He just doesn't have the time.

Star quality to Jeff Greenberg is a combination of talent and a sense of danger in actors. "It's who they are in life, and when they translate it into the role they're playing, they bring an aliveness to it that makes it special, unique, and riveting."

Harriet Greenspan

NBC Productions
330 Bob Hope Dr., Trailer F
Burbank, CA 91523
(818) 526-2720

I actually fell into casting," admits Harriet Greenspan, working on *Sunset Beach* for Aaron Spelling Productions. "In the old days, producers did the casting. So when I was growing up, I didn't say, 'Oh, I want to be a casting director!'" Instead, she graduated from college with a major in drama and was lucky enough to have an uncle who was one of the writer/producers of *Barney Miller*. "I was hired as a receptionist, but not long after I arrived, the casting director quit, her assistant moved into her spot, and I became assistant casting director. It was very exciting. I never even knew this existed!"

Having had a taste of casting, Greenspan decided to get the best mentoring possible and went to work for Lynn Stalmaster, "a master of the game," she says. "I started at the bottom, doing contracts, learning the rules and regulations, and, finally, reading actors and doing the actual casting." Four years later she was hired as a full-fledged casting director by ABC Television, where she remained until she got married and moved to New York. There she wound up primarily doing commercials, and she didn't enjoy it as much.

Greenspan moved back to Los Angeles. "For six months, I shuttled back and forth looking for a job, until I finally hooked up with Annette Benson, with whom I partnered for a year." But when Benson opted for a staff position, as opposed to remaining independent, Greenspan had to begin her search anew. She feels very fortunate to have landed the job at Spelling. "I'm grateful for this opportunity," she declares. "It's wonderful. I never thought I'd get a soap. I cast two roles on a soap for NBC, and they asked me if I wanted to do it full time. It's perfect for me. I'm able to do two outside projects a year. I'm ten minutes from my house, and they don't bug me."

Greenspan enjoys being able to give

> CREDITS INCLUDE:
> *Sunset Beach*
> *Gun*
> *Love Deadly Triangle*
> *She's Leaving Home*
> *Touched by Evil*

actors opportunities. "I'm sensitive to actors. I've been out there fighting for jobs myself, and it's not easy. I love sitting and schmoozing with actors. When actors come into my office, I give them every shot I can." She can tell pretty quickly if they have potential. "I can see if they're right for something, and if they don't get it perfectly the first time, I'll sit and work with them. I'll even give them a line reading if I have to. Even though I'm very busy, I feel everyone deserves the best shot." She believes that's what sets her apart from many other casting directors. "If an agent says I've got to see so-and-so, he's terrific, I'll squeeze him in. You never know. Even the smallest agents may have the best people."

Further evidence of Greenspan's sensitivity to actors is that she'll bring an actor back even if he or she doesn't do a great job at an audition. Six months down the line, the actor may have improved, and she'll give him the benefit of the doubt. "Also, if I have actors in to read, and they don't get the job, I'll give them an opportunity to read for me or for the producers on another project. I tell them I'll be glad to help them get the job, even though I know actors don't like to come back once I've seen them. But if they need coaching, I'm there for them."

She believes it's in her best interest to make sure her actors are fully prepared. "It's your reputation on the line, and you want your producer to say, 'I just don't know whom to choose. They're all so terrific!'"

For *Sunset Beach*, Greenspan hires lots of actors as day players. She also casts recurring characters. She recalls one actress, a former Miss USA, who recently came in to read for the part of a flirtatious character. "I didn't expect her to be very good, and she was terrific. So, we combined two roles into one and used her several times. They liked her so much they wrote her in as a recurring character." And, unlike most network TV shows, *Sunset Beach* is cast by Greenspan without producer approval for most of the roles. "In a way, it pays a great compliment to a casting director to trust her that much. But it's causes a lot of pressure. I have to read twice as many people. I need to make sure I'm hiring the best possible person for the role. That's a big thing for me."

She doesn't stop once the role is cast. She'll work with actors unfamiliar with daytime until they feel really comfortable. "I know once they get on the set they get little direction. They'll be told where to stand and then walk through it a couple of times. So I work with them until I feel confident that when they leave my office they're three-quarters ready to go on."

She also works with actors during casting workshops. "It's a great way to find people. Every workshop is different. I give them sides from *Sunset Beach,* and they have about twenty minutes to look it over. Depending on the time, we do fun things like mix and match, where three people prepare a scene and change roles. I want actors to know that auditioning is very tough and always different. When an actor reads for a producer, it's not going to be the same as it was at home practicing it with a brother or sister. It all depends on whom you're reading with, where you're reading, and even what day it is."

Greenspan is an advocate of showcases, too. She believes an actor must have exposure. "Nobody is going to hire you without seeing something you've done. Work during the day, and do your show-cases and stuff at night," she suggests. "That's the perfect way to do it until you get discovered. It'll happen one way or the other. You have to be patient."

But keep your options open, she adds. "We all need choices. Without choices, we're desperate and unhappy. Nobody likes not having control over his or her life, and if you're backed into a cor-ner, you get frustrated and angry." Getting out there and talking to people and being attentive are all positives, she says. "Don't just walk around saying you want to be an actor. Do it! If you have a dream, go out and do it!"

Karen Hendel

KAREN HENDEL CASTING

424 N. Lucerne Blvd.
Los Angeles, CA 90004

Karen Hendel has, more than once, put her job on the line to secure the right actors for a specific project. There were several times she expected to lose her position as head of casting for HBO when she stood up for what she thought was the best choice. For instance, when she was working on *The James Brady Story*, she was convinced Beau Bridges would be perfect for the lead. Others at the cable network didn't agree. They wanted a bigger name. It took them three months, she says, to concede. "And even then," she adds, "they told me, 'This is on your head, Karen!'" Bridges went on to win an Emmy.

Another case in point was *Dead Man Out*, about a man on death row and a psychiatrist. The network brass were hoping for a Kevin Kline or William Hurt, but actors in that celebrity bracket were apparently not available or not interested in the project. "I suggested interracial casting. There was nowhere in the script that indicated the guys had to be Caucasian, and I thought Danny Glover and Ruben Blades would be wonderful in the roles. Well, I was warned not to pursue this idea, but I did, and the film won all sorts of awards at the film festivals."

A woman of conviction, Hendel advises actors to be determined. She is convinced that about 70 percent of the job is the audition. The single most important piece of advice she imparts to actors is to avoid seeing themselves as victims. "If you come in as a victim," she explains, "I can tell, and so can most casting directors. If you come in so scared you don't have any freedom, you can't possibly act." She feels that the basic problem most actors have is thinking that *this* job will save or change their lives. "Don't come in desperate and with a chip on your shoulder because you don't

CREDITS INCLUDE:
Stalin U.S. casting
The Josephine Baker Story HBO
Barbarians at the Gate HBO
The James Brady Story HBO
The Simon Wiesenthal Story
U.S. casting

like auditions," she says. An actor looking for validation is simply missing the mark. "This is not a business for personal validation, because most of the time you're going to be rejected. That's just the nature of the business."

Hendel hopes an actor can get involved with outside activities so that the audition doesn't become the most important thing in life. "There are too many variables," she says. "We don't make personal judgments at an audition. It's a choice the director makes. Maybe there are already three blondes in the film, and I cannot go with another blonde, or maybe it's something in the script where you have to look like the woman who's already set to play your mother, or forty years old, or Italian. There are so many things to take into consideration, and an actor has to understand that."

Hendel hopes actors will ask questions at an audition, so she can get a sense of who they are and make them feel more comfortable prior to their readings. "I often find it rather shocking when someone doesn't have questions. The actors who come in and say they have no questions, nine times out of ten don't know what they're doing."

Hendel relies mainly on agent submissions, "which, I would say, for a two-hour movie is probably about three or four thousand pictures." Looking through every one that comes in, she examines the résumés for credits and training. Having taught acting at UCLA, she regards training as a vital part of an actor's duty.

If an actor refuses to pre-read for Hendel, she'll refuse to bring him or her in to read for the director or producer. "What most actors don't seem to understand," she says, "is that every time I bring an actor in to see a director, I'm saying I think this person is right for the job. I'm not going to put my reputation on the line by bringing in somebody whose work I don't know." And if an agent says his client doesn't pre-read, Hendel simply responds, "Then your actor doesn't see the director."

Hendel's auditions often take longer than ten minutes, because she feels it her duty to get what she needs out of an actor. As for the number of people per role, she tries to limit it to eight.

She does not expect actors to memorize the material and prefers that they don't. "You're giving the wrong message to the director and producer: that it's a finished performance." She suggests, instead, that an actor be very familiar with the material, but always hold that piece of paper in his or her hand. "You may forget the lines. Why give yourself that added pressure?"

The Hendel dress code is strictly untheatrical. "I take it as a personal insult if somebody comes in wearing a costume. That's telling me they don't think I have any imagination. If you're playing a lawyer, I don't need to see you in a suit. I've had people read for me for army roles who've come in wearing full camouflage. It turns me off."

Another thing she dislikes are cold reading workshops. "I don't think cold readings have anything to do with acting. If actors have some problems auditioning and go to cold reading classes thinking they're studying acting, they're fooling themselves. They're studying how to audition, which has nothing to do with acting. They're separate issues."

Hendel was responsible for several prominent actors getting their SAG cards, including John Malkovich, Amy Madigan, and Julia Roberts. Talent and confidence are primary considerations to this casting director; it doesn't matter whether or not the actors in question are in the union. If she has to, she'll hire them on the basis of the Taft-Hartley Act (see page 30)—they just have to be good.

If you're a good actor and want Hendel to see you, there's no better place than onstage. Doing as much theater as possible also shows her just how devoted you are to practicing your craft. "Would you expect Itzhak Perlman to get onstage without having done his scales for the last six months?" she asks. "An actor, too, has an instrument—a physical, emotional body—and you have to take care of it as you would a Stradivarius."

Judy Henderson

JUDY HENDERSON & ASSOCIATES

Associates: Alycia Aumuller, Robyn Levinson
330 West 89th St.
New York, NY 10024
(212) 877-0225
FAX (212) 724-1620

Judy Henderson has a diverse business in New York, incorporating theater, film, and commercial casting and excelling at each. "Most of the work we've done we haven't had to seek. People have come to us," she says. "They've heard about us through our reputation or seen our work, and they'll call and ask us to read their scripts and take meetings. I haven't really had to do mailings and things like that to pursue clients."

Henderson and her associate, Alycia Aumuller, have been casting since 1984. Prior to that, Henderson worked for an advertising agency as a casting director. "What attracts me to this profession is the creative part of watching actors stretch and change their qualities for different projects. It's a field in which I have more freedom, and also it's more ongoing than, say, directing or producing."

Henderson's approach to casting is not radically different from that of her colleagues. "We'll read a script, consider who might be interesting in each role, and try to get the actor away from the printed page. In other words, I want the actor to give me a range of possibilities, not just stick to what the writer has set down in words." That's not to say you shouldn't aim to please the writer and director, she remarks. "But you want to open it up a little more, because sometimes your most interesting casting comes from that." An example is the casting of Kevin Conway in the play *Other People's Money*. "The part was written for a six-foot-three, very big guy, and we wound up with Kevin, who is pretty short. They laughed at me when I first talked about him, because he was so different from the original concept of the

CREDITS INCLUDE:
Suburbia
Before Sunrise
Pompatus of Love
Other People's Money Theater
Salome Theater
Ecstasy Theater

character. But he was a fabulous actor with quality in his choices. I thought he would make the part exciting and special, and he did. He got the reviews of the season." And the icing on the cake was an apology from the author. "He sent me a wonderful letter that said 'I was wrong. You were right.'"

Henderson finds she has to make some adjustments in her approach to casting when she's doing a film, versus a play. "In terms of the abilities of the actors, it's the same. But when you're doing theater it involves the projection space and big choices. In the theater you have to fill a huge space, and people who are not trained theatrically find it very difficult. Film casting is more intimate. Actors have to bring everything in as opposed to bringing everything out. But in the end, good work is good work."

Most of Henderson's casting is done in New York, but occasionally she travels to Los Angeles. "When we were working on the Broadway production of Wilde's *Salome,* starring Al Pacino, I cast in both cities. We wanted to find some 'name' actors. It was a very difficult role. We saw some really wonderful young women in L.A. We ultimately chose Sheryl Lee for the female lead."

Henderson is of the opinion that an actor should be well trained. "Actors will grow more in their craft if they know how to make choices, break down a script, and understand the written word more thoroughly. They are then able to bring more than just their personalities to a piece. Especially in theater, you have to be able to channel natural talent, and training does that."

When she's casting for film and looking at pictures and résumés, she concentrates more on the photo. "Theater is a visual medium, too, but it's not as structured on physicality as it is on ability. An actor onstage doesn't have to be as beautiful as an actor in film. You don't get as close to the actor on stage. You have that distance, and makeup makes a huge difference in theater." Henderson focuses her attention more on the résumé when casting for the stage. "Of course, if I need a twenty-one-year-old, I won't bring in someone who looks sixty."

The schools Henderson admires most for training include Juilliard, New York University, North Carolina School of the Arts, and Yale. "For film," she says, "the Neighborhood Playhouse, in New York, does a very good job, and Rutgers is great for film and theater."

Doing commercials, she feels, is a good way to get experience, and since her office does lots of commercial casting, she has helped actors make the transition into film. "I found Jason Alexander when he was twentyish," she recalls. "One of his first jobs was a

voiceover for us. He's always been a brilliant actor and performer."
Henderson also recalls Ron Eldard coming for a commercial audition prior to his being cast in *Men Behaving Badly*. "Commercial experience really helps," Henderson explains. "It gives performers a way of dealing with the audition process so they don't melt when they get into stronger, more visual situations."

Henderson will meet actors on general interviews. "I want to find out what kind of personality you have; how you handle yourself in a professional situation; if you're well groomed; if you're on time; where you've trained. I want to find out if you're shy or outgoing." As for talent, she says, "I've been fooled. One actor I met was very outgoing and good with small roles that didn't require a lot of camera or stage time. And physically she was right for the thing we were casting, which was a stage piece. We brought her in, and she was embarrassingly bad. She just couldn't cut it. It was an eye-opener for me. She just didn't have the training."

So if you want to make an impression on this casting director don't make an appointment to see her until you're really ready. Get the proper training. Get some experience. Then set up the general.

Marc Hirschfeld

LIBERMAN/HIRSCHFELD CASTING

Partner: Meg Liberman
4311 Wilshire Blvd. #606
Los Angeles, CA 90010
(213) 525-1381
FAX (213) 525-0131

It's not important to Marc Hirschfeld, who casts some of the most popular shows on television, whether or not actors have an agent. "If they're right for the part, I'll hunt them down and find them," he asserts. A case in point is Wayne Kennedy, a standup comic from Chicago: "I called him up and said, 'You don't know me, but I hear you're really funny and may be right for a series regular. If you're interested, would you put yourself on tape?' I sent him the script. Wayne taped the audition and sent it to us. We ended up flying him to Los Angeles for a test option."

Kennedy didn't get the part, but he did get an overall deal with Columbia for his own show. "It's an emotional and financial investment for some actors, but I think if you seriously want to be considered for the Los Angeles market, you have to be willing to take risks. Otherwise, you might languish in Boston or Cleveland for a long time."

Hirschfeld looks for confidence, intelligence, and a well-rounded character in an actor. Having worked on casting for *Seinfeld*, he is always on the prowl for an inventive and original actor. The ability to take direction is a prime requisite as well. There have been instances where a producer has changed a role to suit the script, and an actor who can't be flexible will simply wind up being replaced by a more accommodating talent. Hirschfeld believes most actors want direction, but some who are more insecure take it personally. "If you take it personally, then become a director, not an actor," he advises.

He also cautions actors against changing lines during a reading.

CREDITS INCLUDE:
Seinfeld
Grace Under Fire
The Larry Sanders Show
Third Rock from the Sun
Married...with Children
Alien Nation TV movie

"Usually the producers you're auditioning for are writers, and writers are very sensitive about their words. Each word is individually placed, just so, and actors who come in and rewrite it get comments like 'If I'd wanted a writer, I would have hired one!'" (He does admit, however, that in one instance a producer was so impressed by an alteration an actor made in the dialogue he asked, 'If we don't hire you, can we buy that?'") Hirschfeld also feels an actor should make decisions before coming into the room and not ask the director whether to sit or stand or move around. It's part of an actor's choice, just as the interpretation of the character is.

Hirschfeld will consider an individual with raw talent, but he prefers dealing with a trained actor. "You can see raw talent, but it's either going to take experience, repeated auditioning, or some serious study to fine-tune and hone that talent."

When he cast the pilot for *Married ... with Children,* several cast members had little television experience. They were trained in theater. He spotted Katie Sagal at the Pasadena Playhouse, and when Sam Kinison turned down the role of Al Bundy, Hirschfeld thought of Ed O'Neil, whom he'd seen at the Hartford Stage in Connecticut doing Lenny in *Of Mice and Men.* O'Neil was the complete antithesis of Kinison, but his "gentle giant" quality intrigued everyone.

Not only does Hirschfeld frequent the theater in New York and L.A., but he also visits San Francisco, Chicago, and Dallas to scout talent. He attends the League of Resident Theatres Lottery Auditions in New York, featuring the graduating classes of Yale and Juilliard, and is invited to Northwestern for performances by its graduating class.

While Hirschfeld has little time for phone chats with actors, he does appreciate them sending a postcard letting him know if they're appearing on TV or the stage. And despite the frustrations actors may feel facing one rejection after another, Hirschfeld advises them to "leave it all behind" at an audition. "Just go in there and don't second-guess yourself or say, 'Oh, my God, I'm one of ten people sitting out in the hallway.' Producers aren't thinking like that. They want to cast the role. They have better things to do than sit there and read actors. You just have to go in there with the attitude, 'I'm the one!'"

Billy Hopkins

Partners: Suzanne Smith, Kerry Barden
Associates: Jennifer McNamara, Mark Bennett
19 Jay St.
New York, NY 10013
(212) 966-6000
FAX (212) 966-5604

Billy Hopkins has been casting long enough to know whether an actor is talented the moment he or she walks into the room. "I just know, believe me. I've only been wrong once. The actress was great at callbacks, but once we got into rehearsals she couldn't handle it. That's not to say there haven't been actors I've cast who weren't good, but I was aware at the time that I was taking a risk."

Because he possesses this insight, he prefers to meet with actors rather than have them read for him right away, and he never asks actors to come into his office with a prepared monologue. "I don't need to see that. I consider myself different from other casting directors in that I much prefer talking to people about their families and where they grew up than about acting."

Hopkins will set up a meeting with an actor if a photo catches his eye or an agent suggests the actor for a particular part. If the person seems right for a role, Hopkins will then set up an audition. If he's impressed with an actor but sees no appropriate role at the moment, he'll keep him or her in mind for the future. Although he says he doesn't discriminate between film and television actors, he says there are some who have a hard time auditioning for one medium if they're used to reading for another. "A good theater actor can act in any medium, but there are some film actors who couldn't act onstage even if their lives depended on it—they don't have the technique or the training." He laments that there are so many good theater actors who get scarcely enough work in film because

CREDITS INCLUDE:
The Last Days of Disco
Home Alone 3
Seven
Six Degrees of Separation
Roseanne
Bad Girl Music video
A Streetcar Named Desire
Broadway revival

of their looks. "They're not considered pretty in the Hollywood sense."

But he will hire actors he's seen onstage even though they may not be "pretty" or may have little camera experience. He loves New York stage actors and has helped many a career blossom, including that of Laurie Metcalf. "We saw her in the theater, and then we cast her in *Desperately Seeking Susan* and a number of films since then." Another actress who owes her start to Hopkins is Ellen Barkin, whom he hired for an off-Broadway play years ago.

Hopkins usually reads with the actors at auditions. If the production will pay for a reader he won't object, for he admits he's not an actor. "I do think an actor should be able to read against anybody, though I often think a reader may sometimes throw an actor off, and that we can be more helpful than a reader." Actors usually read only once for him, then do a callback for the director. If Hopkins knows an actor's work, he'll probably skip the first reading and send the actor on to the director right away. "I work differently with everybody. Some directors like to see everything on videotape first. For example, Clint Eastwood supposedly never sees anybody in person. I don't cast for him, but he does it all by tape."

Hopkins isn't against the use of videotape for audition purposes, but he does think that not all directors are equally adept at using it. "I worked with one director who hardly read anyone. He just had me film the meetings with the actors, and he would simply call in the actors he was interested in and do an improv with them based on a situation that had nothing to do with the script. It is possible to cast that way, but only if you trust your instincts. I mean, that's what casting really is."

Hopkins feels he has more autonomy on a film project than he has with a theatrical one. "Many times, with the smaller parts, stage directors will simply trust you, but when it comes to the bigger roles, they'll often use the same people over and over. At Lincoln Center [where he cast for six years] we had a company of actors we used time and again. When I'm doing a film, the director usually wants new faces, and you have to keep looking until you find the right ones."

But Hopkins enjoys researching his films. He does it all the time when working for director Oliver Stone. "I knew nothing about Jim Morrison or the Doors before I started working on the Morrison project, but within a couple of weeks, I knew everything there was to know about them. You do your homework." Hopkins made sure he studied the Stock Exchange before tackling *Wall Street*, and he made frequent trips to a veterans' hospital while researching *Born on the 4th of July*.

Authenticity is important to Hopkins. He will often cast real people in certain roles, such as attorney William Kunstler in *The Doors*, Abbie Hoffman in *4th of July*, and several financial people in *Wall Street*. "You have to balance it, though, with experienced actors, because you cannot cast a movie with only real people and expect it to be professional."

When Madonna was cast in *Desperately Seeking Susan*, she had never acted before, and when she did *Speed-the-Plow*, it was her first time on the theatrical stage. "She loved David Mamet's work, and her audition was just as good as anybody's. In fact, the woman who took over the role was equally good—a then-unknown actress named Felicity Huffman."

Casting someone based on ethnic suitability is something Hopkins finds disagreeable. Kevin Kline portrayed a Cuban in *Mambo Kings*. "I think Kline was brilliant in the role," says Hopkins, "and you ultimately go with the best actor, no matter what nationality he is. The controversy over Jonathan Pryce in *Miss Saigon* was ridiculous. I was a little disappointed in Brad Wong, who put up all the fuss; I brought Brad in for a movie that wasn't written for an Asian, and I never thought twice about it." For *Jacob's Ladder*, Hopkins brought in Elizabeth Peña to play the lead, even though the part was not originally intended for a Hispanic. "The other major contenders included Julia Roberts and Madonna. It was actually considered a risk when we cast Peña in the role."

Hopkins likes to think of himself as a man who takes risks, and he's well respected for the risks he takes. He, in turn, respects actors and encourages them to take chances, too. If there's one thing he appreciates most, however, it's tact. "I always remember an actor who says thank you."

Stuart Howard

STUART HOWARD ASSOCIATES, LTD.

Associates: Amy Schecter, Howard Meltzer
22 W. 27th St., 10th floor
New York, NY 10001
(212) 725-7770
FAX (212) 725-7389

O kay," sighs veteran casting director Stuart Howard, "I'll tell you the long story of how my career began." And it's quite a story. Howard obtained his master's degree in drama from Purdue University after completing his undergrad work at Carnegie Mellon University. From there it was on to Paris where he studied French classical drama at the Sorbonne. "It was even more adventurous than I'd dreamed," he relates, "because they refused to speak one word of English. So I sat there for a good solid three months without understanding one tenth of what was being taught!" Until one day he was listening to a lecture, and all of a sudden he realized he understood what was being said. "It was like a light going on. It just suddenly sank in."

With a desire to direct, Howard began job-hunting on his return to New York. "I couldn't get work as a director, so I became an agent, and the strangest thing happened to me. I got a phone call, and I have no idea who referred this person to me, but I can tell you it changed my life. The head of personnel at Ogilvy & Mather called to see if I'd like to be a casting director. I had never worked on a single commercial! I had never even set foot in an advertising agency!"

Howard got the job and worked there five years, at which time he and his best friend, Louie Pulzino, decided to open their own casting office.

One year after they opened their office, Louie was killed by a truck on Central Park West. "I thought of closing the office, and then two other friends called. They were going to be the executive producers of a show they want-

CREDITS INCLUDE:
Chicago Broadway/Touring
Grease! Broadway/Touring
Annie Broadway/Touring
Death Defying Acts Off-Broadway
Cinderella TV

ed me to cast. It turned out to be *La Cage Aux Folles.* It was amazing. The very first day of auditions we saw George Hearn, and the very last day Gene Barry auditioned. It's still the best experience I've ever had. It ran for five years on Broadway, and we got to do it all over the world."

George Hearn might not have even had a chance to audition but for Howard: "The main producer of *La Cage* warned me not to bring him in. I was never given a reason, but I knew if I thwarted him, my job was on the line. I brought George in anyway—I don't think I'd ever been that brave—but I didn't know anyone else who could do the role as well. Well, the producer never opened his mouth, but the director, Arthur Laurents, stood up in front of everyone and said 'We are never going to do any better than this. Hire him.'"

When casting a play, Howard and his associates make a "wish list" of stars they'd like to approach. They make other lists for the supporting roles that don't require name talent. "We then use our files, and I don't necessarily mean photos and résumés but lists of actors we've auditioned before. We have a copy of every single audition we ever held. From the beginning, Amy Schecter has kept the history of this office in huge black binders, and every time we do an audition we three-hole punch our notes for the file. When the show is done, Amy labels it and puts it away." Then, when a new show is being cast, they all go through the extensive files. "For instance, in casting a new national tour and Broadway production of *Dreamgirls,* a show which is 99-percent African-American, we went through the notes of other shows in which we cast African-American singers and dancers. It really helps." They also rely on agents with whom they've worked to supply them with lists of actors.

"I take special pride in finding new people," he says. "Anytime someone I respect asks us to meet someone terrifically talented, we will always do that. We go to showcases, plays, schools."

The next step is the auditioning process, and just as with feature film and television, Howard and his associates may do a lot of pre-screening of actors before taking them to the producers. "The director may only want to see four people for a role, so we'll see twenty-four." And the numbers multiply if it's a Broadway production. "We're required to see any member of Equity who wishes to audition during the mandatory three days of Equity calls for any first-class production. Aside from the consideration of talent, most of the time the people coming in aren't right for the roles, but that is never taken into consideration. They're union members, and their union demands that we audition them." Howard isn't against open calls, but he feels that 75 percent or more are a waste of time for everyone concerned. "Should we have open calls?" he asks. "Absolutely. Should it be for every single project? I don't believe so."

More upsetting to Howard is the reluctance of many fine actors to commit to theater. "They just don't want to be under contract for a long time. Their agents and managers have told them that theater is a stepping-stone to what their real career is—television and movies. Theater is no longer thought of as the top of the ladder by agents and managers; it's considered the bottom rung. And that's real sad as far as I'm concerned. But we simply can't recoup our investment if an actor stays for three months." Actors such as Glenn Close, Julie Andrews, Alec Baldwin, and Kathleen Turner, however, will commit to doing a play, and he's grateful for those few to whom theater is a priority.

His own priority is finding actors who prepared. "So many actors treat the business as if it weren't a business. Do you know how many actors come in to auditions without photos and résumés? They say, 'Oh, my agent will send it over.' And my question to them is, 'Is it too heavy to carry?'" His other bugaboo is actors who—because of nerves or not knowing what to say—start chattering. "Asking inane questions that have nothing to do with the audition. The director just wants to see what they've prepared. I remember one well-known star auditioned for us and literally—believe me, I was looking at my watch—went on chattering for forty-seven minutes! The actor we hired to read with her wound up starting and stopping twelve times."

Howard even teaches a class on how to audition and how to be a more professional actor. "Michael Kahn, head of the drama division at Juilliard, invited me to teach fourth-year students, and it's been one of the joys of my life." And what is one of the most important lessons an actor can learn before he or she heads out into the world? "It's up to you. It is not your agent. It is not your manager. It is not the fault of the casting director that you're not getting work. It's you. It's your job. It's your life. It's your career. You have to do it."

Phyllis Huffman

Associate: Olivia Harris
1324 Ave. of the Americas
New York, NY 10019
(212) 636-5023
FAX (212) 636-5055

The really important thing about casting," says Phyllis Huffman, "is creating a place for actors when they come in to audition. The actor should know that he or she is the most important person here." She makes every effort to let actors know that her office is a welcoming, tranquil place, and that she wants them to get the part. "That atmosphere is created from the minute he or she steps off the elevator and comes into my reception area. When someone comes into the inner office to meet the director and producer, it's my job to make it as nonthreatening as possible so they can see what they have to see in a very short time."

It's not that she feels superior to other casting directors, but Huffman is aware that it's a very powerful position and that some casting directors tend to take advantage of that. "The people who don't really give a lot of thought or understanding to the idea that it's really about producers and directors get sort of carried away with this power." She admits that the casting process can be a terribly hectic, nerve-racking business with a lot at stake, but after being in the business for so long, she's learned to take the frenzy in stride, to a certain extent.

Huffman makes sure that actors have sides in hand before the audition is scheduled. "They come in, and if I don't know them, haven't seen them work, or haven't read them before, I'll have them read for me before meeting the producer or director. We'll just read the scene together, and then I'll decide if they should come in and read for the others."

CREDITS INCLUDE:
Midnight in the Garden of Good and Evil
Absolute Power
Private Parts
Unforgiven
Old Man Hallmark
The Boys Next Door Hallmark
Miss Rose White TV movie

Because she lets actors know the script is available ahead of time, she expects them to be well prepared. "I think that's the best thing an actor can do. The competition is fierce. The volume of actors is staggering. As an actor, you get one shot when you walk in the door." The rest of the impression an actor creates is about who he or she is. "There's a sense of confidence that comes in the door with an actor, and that comes from studying, being up on your feet in a class or in different situations—being somebody who takes it quite seriously and works at it, even when you're not at an audition or in a professional situation."

Huffman finds her actors through the usual channels: pictures, directories, and agents. But she also makes use of her invaluable associate, Olivia Harris, who scours the New York theater. "She has this gift. You could line up maybe ten people whom nobody knows, and she could always pick out the good one. She's at the theater every night." That's how they discovered John Finn. "Olivia had brought him to me a year before he got cast as the Irish drill sergeant in *Glory*. We used him for a bit part on *Hawk* after seeing him do some little off-Broadway play."

There are times when Huffman will think she's discovered a winner, only to find she's been gravely mistaken. "It was my first pilot at Warner Brothers in 1982. I had just been made vice president of television casting, and I went over to CBS with five fabulous actors to play the third lead in *Murphy Brown*. It was an enormous part. This one fellow was wonderful at the auditions, better than all the others. I don't know what it was, but when we saw the dailies, he was terrible. And the worst thing about it, it was a comedy! This one particular actor could be funny, but the script didn't call for people who could be funny—it needed funny people." That experience taught Huffman a valuable lesson about comedy, something Juliet Taylor keeps in mind when she's casting with Woody Allen. You must make us laugh without even opening your mouth or you're not really funny.

That kind of authenticity is a big plus with Huffman. "If you go back to the people who just knock you out, in every case they're the genuine article." She cites Marg Heldenberger of *China Beach* as an example. "Her agent really kept after me to see her. I always liked her, but she wasn't number one on my list. When I finally brought her in at the persuasion of her agent, I was wowed and immediately brought her to the producers. They hired her right on the spot."

It wasn't only that actor's authenticity, although that quality was there, but it was what Huffman calls her "grit" and amazing versatility. There are some actors Huffman would never think twice about bringing in for either a television or feature film. But there are others whom she feels are right for one medium or the other, not both. "I think their persona may not be big enough for film. They're just not good enough. You've seen many people who've tried to make that crossover from television to movies, and for some reason they just don't hold up on the big screen." That doesn't mean they're not good enough for smaller roles on TV.

Working with Clint Eastwood on most of his films has made up for the occasional disappointments of TV casting. "We've worked together for so long. A couple of times, I've shown him one actor, and he has such terrific casting sense he has said, 'That's it!'" Huffman says many times he'll opt for just a feel or a look about an actor, as opposed to an accomplished technical actor. He's aware of what the camera picks up, and even if he's casting a number of "bad guys," he'll insist that each have a distinctive, dramatic look. "So that they don't get confused. He's very conscious of that, and it's really fun, going out of our way, often sacrificing a great actor to hire someone with this terrific look. As soon as the camera's on him, you know what's going on."

Phyllis Huffman appears to have the best of both worlds: major films and quality television projects. Does she prefer one medium over the other? "No. I know a lot of people who form a pecking order: feature films and then television. A lot of people disregard television, but I like it. It's fast, it's very diverse, and there's an enormous amount of energy that goes into it."

Jane Jenkins & Janet Hirshenson

THE CASTING COMPANY

7461 Beverly Blvd., 5th floor
Los Angeles, CA 90036
(213) 938-0700
FAX (213) 938-9978

It's likely that if Rob Reiner is directing a film, he'll be calling on Jane Jenkins and Janet Hirshenson, a.k.a. the Casting Company, to cast it. They have cast every single movie Reiner has done since *The Sure Thing* (except *Spinal Tap*, which he cast himself). The Casting Company is also the first choice of directors Wolfgang Peterson and Ron Howard. As you might imagine, they're a busy office, casting at least five major films a year. Feature films are their bread and butter, but, having worked on both episodics and miniseries, they do have a somewhat eclectic résumé.

The women come from very different backgrounds and yet seem to complement each other perfectly. Jenkins is from an acting background in New York; Hirshenson worked as a medical assistant. "It probably works," Jenkins explains, "because we've never analyzed it too much. Politically and philosophically, we're alike. We don't impose ourselves on people, and we respect actors."

The two met as assistants for a casting director whom they call their spiritual mother, Jennifer Shull. What works best for them is to create an atmosphere of warmth. "We try to make our office as conducive as possible to good readings," says Hirshenson, "because we want everyone who comes in here to do a great job. If they don't, we just have to keep on looking."

Most of the parts they cast are day players, which are often difficult for actors."A lot of those parts are a couple of lines," Hirshenson explains. "The actors want to show their best work, when all we want is

CREDITS INCLUDE:
In Dreams
My Favorite Martian
Air Force One
Lost World
Ghosts of Mississippi

someone to come in and just do it. They want to give it their all, but that's not what the scene is usually about. It's probably about somebody else, and a simple reading is all that's required."

Jenkins recounts an audition a couple of years ago for *Outbreak*: "This young actress had two lines, no more than four words in each sentence. It was an emotional moment, because her boyfriend in the script is dying, and she's at his bedside saying, 'Henry, you have to fight.' This is a job the actress desperately wants. How does she convey this dramatic moment with a few words?" The simpler you are, Jenkins advises, the more real you are, and the more impact it's going to have. "It's so hard to do, but we both look for actors who trust themselves to keep it as simple as possible." They encourage actors to take the pressure off, instead of investing too much. "We let them go crazy if they want to the first time. Then, the second time, we say 'Let's just do it once more, a little easier.'"

Actors must be realistic about the casting process. Just because an actor makes a great impression on Jenkins or Hirshenson doesn't mean that actor will be cast. "I remember when we met Liam Neeson," Hirshenson recalls. "It was on a general, and he wanted to read for the part of the giant in *The Princess Bride*," Jenkins recalls. "I told him he may be tall, but not tall enough for this. He came in again for *Beetlejuice*, but he wasn't right for that either. His American accent just wasn't American enough. It's one thing to recognize talent, but it's that serendipity, when an actor finds himself at the right place at the right time, that makes him a star."

Good training and respectable credits are impressive, but to Jenkins and Hirshenson the look is of primary importance. "If it's just another pretty face," says Janet, "there are eight hundred coming in. We're looking for very specific types."

Jenkins remembers her dilemma when casting *Mystic Pizza*. The part of a young Portuguese waitress just wouldn't get cast. They'd had dozens of young actresses come in to read, but no one was right. Then Julia Roberts appeared. "She hadn't done her homework," Jenkins recalls. "She hadn't read the script. She didn't look the part at all. And yet there was a quality about her that was really right. I stopped her soon after she began and asked her why she hadn't read the script. She said she'd been too busy. I told her to go home, read it, and come back the next day. I also told her she looked about as Portuguese as I did, and she asked me what Portuguese people looked like. Well, she came back the next day with dark hair, dressed more appropriately for the role, and read the script. She knew what the part was all about, and she nailed it."

If there's one no-no the two casters agree upon, it's "Don't bring props! I hate props!" Jenkins declares. "I had a kid in for a reading who brought a bottle of Pepsi and a bag of potato chips. He no sooner started the scene when the bottle sprayed all over everybody and the chips went flying. There was no way to recover, and everybody just sat there mopping up the pop and feeling like idiots." It was a callback for a lead on a network show, and the incident destroyed any chance for the young man.

Another warning: Don't put casting directors on the spot by asking when callbacks are. "Ask your agent," Hirshenson suggests. "If you think you're going to be out of town, tell your agent, whose job it is to tell you. We've noticed that those who usually ask are those who didn't do a good reading, and it puts everyone on the spot."

The simplest advice they offer: Be yourself. The women's philosophy, borrowed from Ron Howard, is that ninety percent of the actor's work is in getting the job. They feel that the audition is the work process, and getting the job is the reward. "So you come in and do the best you can," says Janet. "You do your best work in an environment that's conducive to bringing out your best."

And you might as well get used to it, because, she adds, "I don't think you ever stop auditioning."

Geoffrey Johnson

JOHNSON-LIFF CASTING ASSOCIATES

Partner: Vincent Liff
Associates: Tara Rubin, Ron LaRosa, Andrew Zerman
1501 Broadway, Suite 1400
New York, NY 10036
(212) 391-2680
FAX (212) 840-0691

If musical theater is your dream and you've got talent, you'll definitely want to be noticed by Johnson-Liff. Geoffrey Johnson and Vincent Liff have been casting Broadway musicals for more than twenty years and have become authorities in that theatrical genre. Johnson admits his office has been type-cast, "even though we never deliberately selected musicals as our specialty when we began. I'm not knocking it," he insists, "but we got labeled 'the musical mavens.'" With the success of *Cats*, *Les Miserables*, and *Phantom*, Johnson-Liff is a hot commodity on Broadway.

Not only do they cast the original productions, but they're put on retainer by the producers to do all the replacement companies across the country. "When we cast the original show we work closely with the director, writers, composers, and producers. We get a good idea of what they want during the audition process. Then, when we're hired to find replacements, we know exactly what they're looking for and bring the appropriate talent to the production supervisor, who's assigned to maintain a specific show." Although it seems that they're dealing with a lot of "cooks," Johnson says it's not as many as he's had to deal with in television. "I'm not knocking television in any way, but theater somehow seems to lend itself to more cooperation. With television, there's the network, the packager, plus all the creative people. When you get fifteen different opinions from fifteen different sources, you're bound to get confused. Some-

CREDITS INCLUDE:
Les Miserables Broadway/Touring
Cats Broadway/Touring
Phantom of the Opera Broadway/Touring
Sister Act
Soul Man
Another World

one will say that girl's not pretty enough. The other will say she's too pretty. When you're casting theater, you don't run into that as often."

While it may be easier on the casting director, it's certainly a lot harder for an actor to get a job in musical theater on Broadway. "The days are gone forever when a dancer only had to dance, and a singer only had to sing. Now, if they're looking for dancers, they have to sing as well as act. You have to be a 'triple threat.'

"With film, if an actor has an interesting personality or face, the training and talent aren't as significant, at least at the beginning. Of course, if an actor wants a future in the business, training and talent are ultimately vital ingredients."

Auditioning for musical theater is intensive. According to Johnson, "auditioning is perhaps ninety percent of an actor's work. I wish there were a better way of doing it, but I haven't been able to come up with an alternative in all the years I've been casting.

"The majority of actors don't audition very well. They don't always show themselves off to their best ability. They'll perhaps decide what the producer is looking for, without having a clue, and that's very bad. Actors will talk among themselves and try to second-guess the director. You can't. You should just go in, read your scene, sing your song, and do your best. Present yourself the best way you know how. Don't listen to other people. Just listen to what the director or casting director tells you. You'll be a lot better off."

Although it depends on the show, most auditions begin with singing. You may be called in at eleven in the morning for the first leg of the audition. If the director feels your voice is what's desired, he may ask you to read a scene from the show. "We try to get actors the material ahead of time. I've always told them never to read cold. If you haven't had time to look over the material, you have every right to ask to step outside for fifteen minutes." If the director is pleased with the reading, the actor may be asked to return later that afternoon for a dance audition.

It's an involved process and quite time-consuming, and sometimes an actor may be wonderful in one area and not so good in another. What then? "We've had actors who sing gloriously and read extremely well, but when they've come back to dance, they're a little weak. I've seen actors hired when the director and choreographer agree that the dancing isn't as vital for that particular character. It doesn't happen often, but it has occurred."

Film and television actors often don't get the chance to audition for a project, simply because their agent hasn't submitted them. It's a different situation for stage actors, who belong to Actors Equity Association. There are usually three days of Equity principal auditions at which anyone in that union can be seen for a particular show. "It never ceases to amaze me," says Johnson, "that as long as I've been in this business and thought that it's got to reach a diminishing return here somehow—that I've seen every actor in New York—I never see them all. Suddenly I'm seeing hundreds of unknowns, and suddenly there's somebody wonderful, and I say in amazement, 'Where have you been?'" There's always a stream of young actors pouring into New York from every corner of the country, recent graduates hoping to get established, others wanting to get away from a more provincial life. "This is the center of it all, and it makes you feel good that you can bring that new person to the director and say, 'This young lady is new in town and can sing like a dream and act, too.'"

Johnson and Liff frequently make trips out of town to find good talent, especially when they're casting future replacements. "Sometimes we hold auditions in cities like Orlando or Nashville. We'll suddenly need a Grisabella for *Cats*, and the show's going to Omaha; we'll go through our list of Omaha possibilities. We didn't need a Grisabella at the time, but now we do. And that's the way it works."

Johnson implores actors to treat their career as a serious business. "A lot of actors think it's fun and games. It's not. I don't mean you can't have fun—of course you can—but it's a business, like studying for the bar or becoming an architect. What I'm saying is: Keep your wits about you, do your job, and do it well. That's how you'll get ahead."

And he stresses, too, that casting directors are not the enemy. "I've heard actors say they are. It isn't true. We always want the actor to get the job. We couldn't be happier than to see each actor succeed. I tell actors this at every symposium I attend: We want you to be great. We want you to get the job!"

Caro Jones

CARO JONES CASTING

Box 3329
Los Angeles, CA 90078
(213) 664-0460
FAX (213) 664-0463

Caro Jones has been a casting director for more than three decades, having started out casting such television classics as *The Beverly Hillbillies, Petticoat Junction,* and *Love American Style.* Today she concentrates on feature film and remarks how things have changed over the years. Perhaps the biggest change came with the institution of Breakdown Services. "It's changed casting drastically, especially here in Hollywood. It's opened it up to a lot of unqualified people." Whereas in the old days casting directors had to create their own breakdowns, today, she believes, virtually anyone can submit a script to Breakdown and simply wait for agents to engulf them with photos and résumés. Jones, however, still prefers making her own lists and scouting for talent. "I still think there's no substitute for going around and seeing actors work."

Not only has the system changed immensely, but the technical aspect of casting has also evolved over the years. "The electronic world we live in has changed a great deal. We put 99 percent of the actors on videotape today, rather than bring actors back four or five times to read for us." Of course, not all casting directors use videotape to the extent Jones does. She tapes everything. "I do it for all the roles I cast, both in town and on location. Eventually, the director meets with those actors he or she has seen on tape and is considering for a role. It saves the tedious process of elimination: I do it for them."

While most casting directors discourage actors from memorizing their sides, Jones thinks it's in their best interest to do so. "First of all, it's impressive to the director. It shows that you think enough about the part and enough about your work

CREDITS INCLUDE:
State Fair Theater
Entertaining Angels Feature
The Power of One Feature
King Miniseries
The Karate Kid Feature

to spend that extra bit of time and energy on the material. Also, if you don't have a script in front of you, you're going to do a better job. There's just no substitute for it." Jones makes sure an actor has access to the sides or script hours before the audition. "That's one of the rules of the Screen Actors Guild, but people don't take advantage of it. And if a casting director won't deliver it to you, you can always go to their office and read it." Or there's Showfax, a service that most casting directors use to fax or e-mail sides quickly to actors (for a slight fee to the actor).

When it comes to a substantial part in a film, Jones insists on actors reading the entire script before an audition. "How can you possibly do a motion picture without seeing how your character fits into the whole story? And how can you expect to fully understand the character unless you've read through to the end of the script? You have to know where you are going, otherwise you can't do your job."

Jones always employs a reader at her auditions and expects actors to relate to that reader as they would to the actor to whom they're playing on camera. If there's action involved, the actor may also be required to display his or her skills. When Jones was called upon to cast features such as *Rocky* and *The Karate Kid,* she expected the male actors to be prepared to show off their muscles or physical agility, whatever was required for the part.

"I think a lot of actors suffer dreadfully from nerves when they get to a really big audition, and that's something they have to learn to cope with," Jones remarks. "It's important to try to get as calm as you can without losing your energy." Energy, she feels, is vital to an actor's performance; without it, the performance is dead. If actors feel they've gotten off on the wrong track during an audition, Jones suggests they ask to start over. "My camera person will be glad to run the tape back and start again. A lot of people feel they have to go through the audition to the bitter end, even if they're unhappy with their performance. You have to use your time to your best advantage, not try to be all things to all people."

Jones is most impressed with actors who constantly try to improve their readings. She recalls Patrick Dempsey's audition for *Can't Buy Me Love.* "We were pretty well down to the wire, and I think we had him back five times and put him on tape every one of those times. But each time he came in, he brought something new to the role. He never just settled, but added more. A lot of actors," she adds, "figure if they did something right the first time, they'd better do it exactly that way again. But if the audition was absolutely perfect, then why would I have to call you back? We've got to see something more. You've got to go back into that part and find out what you can add to that character."

While Jones truly believes talent is an inborn quality, she feels that camera training is a must. "An actor has to learn how the different media work. You've got to keep up your technique, and when you're not working, classes are vital." If an actor doesn't know where to turn, she suggests asking other actors or finding out with which coaches the actors they admire studied. For young actors starting out, she encourages training along with doing auditions for as many good agents as they can find. "Just call them and say you'd like to audition. Agents usually hold monthly auditions. You need an agent. It's almost impossible to function without one."

Jones casts a lot of young talent, and they are the toughest challenge she faces. She'll often hold open calls to give actors a chance to display their merits. When she was working on *Gladiators*, she held two open calls, one in New York and one in Chicago. From the nearly one thousand hopefuls, she put two hundred and fifteen on tape. "We had a huge staff, two cameras, twenty-five Guardian Angels, four readers, and several people showing the actors where to go and giving them their sides." About 75 percent of the hundreds they auditioned were eventually cast in the film.

"It's the joy of discovery that thrills me the most," she says. "I love finding real talent and helping to nurture it. I think that's why most of us are in this business, because we get excited by contributing to the artistic process that goes into making a film."

There are times Jones will suggest an actor to a director and the director turns it down—a frustration to a casting director. But then it can be quite satisfying when that actor goes on to stardom. Such was the case many years ago when Jones was casting for television and tried several times, to no avail, to get Warren Beatty considered by the producers. "They kept turning him down, and he gave brilliant readings." She ran into similar roadblocks with George C. Scott and Alan Alda. "You can't let it get you down, because all those people have been turned down. I think it's just a fact of life."

"If you want to be an actor," advises Jones, "you have to work extremely hard to learn your craft, every aspect of it. Hopefully, you have a natural talent to go with it, but if you don't, you just have to work harder. You must be prepared for a lot of rejection along the way, and the rewards have to mean so much to you that you want to take that risk. Because that's what it is—it's a risk every day."

Lynn Kressel

Associate: Karen Gilman
445 Park Ave., 7th floor
New York, NY 10022
(212) 605-9122
FAX (212) 605-9130

Lynn Kressel has the distinction of being the first casting director to win an Emmy. The award was presented for her work on *Lonesome Dove,* a miniseries that entailed a cast of some ninety actors, of which Kressel was responsible for about eighty. As with most films, the major stars were set before the casting director was even brought aboard. But the supporting cast caught the attention of the Academy of Television Arts and Sciences. It was one of those perfect blends that contributed to the overall success of the production.

Kressel recalls her work on *Lonesome Dove* with deep affection and is proud of her "discoveries," such as Chris Cooper, who played July Johnson. "He was an actor who came out of New York. One of the reasons I was hired was to make it a bicoastal cast and bring in some unknown actors. Glenne Headley was another 'unknown' who now has a successful career."

But Kressel refuses to accept all the credit. "It's clearly the director's vision. Ideally, there's a good relationship and process that happens between a casting director and a director. And what a casting director does is try to make the director aware of the possibilities." That was indeed the case with the animated film *Anastasia.* The producers were thinking of hiring Natassia Kinski to provide the voice for the title role, but Kinski apparently wasn't well, and they needed an alternate. That's when Kressel suggested Amy Irving, who wound up portraying the romantic heroine.

Kressel got her start working for Andy Warhol in New York; she helped him cast *Bad.* "I cast that film out of an ad agency I was working for at the time. I loved casting interesting and offbeat faces and personalities. Negotiating the deals was amaz-

CREDITS INCLUDE:
I'm Not Rappaport
Bad Boys
The Odyssey
Lonesome Dove
Law & Order

ing," she recalls. "I'd call up Andy and say, 'This actor wants this credit, and that one wants that.' He'd say, 'What do you think?' I'd say, 'Well, that would look peculiar,' and he would say, 'If it's peculiar, I like it.'"

Kressel has worked for directors who don't mind being surprised by her choices, as well as for some who are extremely rigid. "The most interesting directors are those whose minds are open, who can see possibilties in different actors." After talking with the director, she'll start showing him or her three or four people for each part, trying to correspond to what the director has asked for. Then she'll bring in another couple of actors who do not quite fit the director's specifications, as a contrast. Sometimes the offbeat approach will succeed, at other times the director will stick with their original intent.

The only difference Kressel finds between casting for features and casting for television is the availability of actors. She says it's easier to get talent for theatrical releases than for movies made for TV. There's simply more money in features, and it's still considered more prestigious. "It's convincing the agents that the script is good that's the hardest part of my job. I have to make sure it's the kind of atmosphere that's conducive to the actor, in terms of meeting with the director, and then making sure they'll be available for the shoot."

She would feel equally comfortable bringing in for a feature film any actor she'd hire for a TV project. "I consider the actors I use of the same caliber in both media—absolutely. They're interesting characters. There's a complete crossover."

Kressel feels it's often easier to convince a director to go with an unknown name for a feature than for a television project. "Oftentimes feature directors will take greater chances with unknown talent. They don't have to play it so safe because TV executives aren't involved."

She's been able to get many undiscovered actors their first credits through her inexhaustible search for capable talent across the country. She put Matthew Modine in his first film, *Private School*, back in 1983. "There was no doubt in my mind that he had star quality. There are just people you know who are destined for it—stars waiting to happen." Julia Roberts came in to read for Diane Lane's part in *Lonesome Dove* before her first feature was released. Why didn't she get the role? "It wasn't my decision. I think she would have been wonderful."

Casting against type is a common Kressel practice. When she was casting the pilot for *Law and Order*, she remembers seeing the part of a mayor's assistant in New York written for a white preppie. She decided to bring in Courtney Vance, who transformed the white preppie into a black preppie, and that's how it eventually wound up on the air.

Kressel is rather flexible when it comes to auditions. What actors wear, how they behave, and whether or not they memorize their sides are not her concern. She does feel that asking too many questions of directors may frighten them into not hiring you, and that a positive frame of mind is preferable to a negative one, but she would rather not place any restrictions on an actor.

There is one thing, however, that leaves a sour taste in her mouth: an actor who refuses to read for a director. "Any actor who really wants the part will read for it," she believes. She heard that Glenn Close agreed to read for *Fatal Attraction*. Kressel will sometimes have to convince an actor to read, which she doesn't enjoy. "It means the actor doesn't really want the part." She recalls an audition she attended on Broadway for *Once in a Lifetime*. Meryl Streep was there. "It wasn't her best audition, but she was hired, because the director could see beyond the reading. The most important thing about the process of casting is keeping one's mind open. Consider the possibilities you have, and be willing to talk about stupid ideas. You begin to arrive at the ones that might be really interesting and wonderful, to find the surprises that make things special. That's what it's about—possibilities, exploring. It's about having the confidence and wisdom to look at anything."

Ruth Lambert

WALT DISNEY FEATURE ANIMATION

500 S. Buena Vista St.
Burbank, CA 91521
(818) 560-9192
FAX (818) 560-9128

Ruth Lambert has a very specific niche in the casting community. When she casts films, she doesn't care one iota about an actor's looks. She might very well hire a six-foot performer to play a dwarf, or a five-foot character actor to portray a romantic male lead. Lambert is more concerned with the actor's voice and acting ability as she meticulously casts each Disney animated feature, a tedious but rewarding task that often takes more than two years to complete.

"Animation is a lengthy process," she explains. "The voices come first, and they're constantly changing the dialogue and adding, tracking scenes and tweaking things. Once they record the voices, then the animation starts. It proceeds scene by scene." But despite the length of time it takes to complete an animated feature, Lambert believes there's a lot less pressure than in casting television. "When you do a show like *Seinfeld*, for instance, you have twenty-three minutes and twenty-three parts. That's incredibly difficult. Here, I have a lot of time to find the actors, and I can be really creative, because we're dealing with voices only. Actors you'd never consider for certain roles, because of how they look, may be perfect for me. I can use just about anyone if he or she has a unique vocal quality. The people I work with are very open. If they're looking for a certain type, and I say why not try something a little different, there may be a few kicks and screams, but they're always willing to give it a try."

Lambert knows casting. She's been doing it for about fifteen years, having been recruited by one of the best, Gretchen Rennell, who was at the

CREDITS INCLUDE:
Mulan
Hercules
The Hunchback of Notre Dame
Pocahontas
Tarzan
A Bug's Life
Kingdom of the Sun
Atlantis

time casting the live-action TV miniseries *The Winds of War.* Lambert spent two and a half years with Rennell, who eventually moved to the West Coast. Lambert decided it was time she, too, made a move and was fortunate to be offered a position at Paramount. "No sooner had they transferred me and I was on the plane than they cut the job. It took a day for them to tell me. I cried a lot!" It wasn't long, however, before she was working again, first at CBS, then at Warner Brothers, and finally at Disney, where her title is Director of Casting.

"The best thing about my job," says Lambert, "is that actors don't mind auditioning for us. James Woods auditioned for *Hercules,* which was really exciting. He'd never done animation before. Nearly everyone, with a few exceptions, auditioned for that film"— including the celebrities. Lambert said she saw two hundred actors for the title role alone. "We auditioned a lot of people before Disney decided on Tate Donovan, who auditioned at least twice. He was perfect: very natural, not cartoony, very sweet. He hadn't had previous voiceover experience, but I didn't care. It doesn't matter as long as they're right for the part. There's a misconception that animation is different from live-action. It's not. I hire actors."

The process of casting is a little different in that actors read their lines into a microphone instead of a camera. Sometimes the audition is in a small open room. Other times it's in a closed booth. "I prefer the actor read in a room in front of the producers and director," says Lambert. "I like the process to be as similar to live-action as possible." And, just as with live-action, she and her colleagues go through the tapes and select those that stand out. "We pull those auditions off the tape and relisten to them or put them up against a picture of the character. That way, we can see the picture and hear the voice together." She recalls a recent casting session for *A Bug's Life,* starring Dave Foley, from *Newsradio.* "I'd known him from TV and thought he'd be right for the role. When he was brought in, it was nice, but when we put him up against the picture of the character, it was really great."

Callbacks are rarely used in voiceover casting. "Through the miracle of editing," Lambert explains, "we can actually match the voices on tape without having to call someone back to read with another actor to see how their voices blend. It's a lot different from live-action."

Lambert finds actors through agents and on the stage. "I go to New York a lot, since I'm familiar with the theater there. I know New York actors. When we were doing *Hercules,* and I needed five great singers for the Muses, I went to Broadway. The same was done for *The Little Mermaid*, which I didn't cast." Lambert recalls the casting of Disney's animated *The Hunchback of Notre Dame*: "The directors and I were convinced that Paul Kandel, who'd starred in *Tommy*, on Broadway, would be perfect for Clopin. It took forever, however, to convince some of the other folks to see him in the role. They wanted someone else, but I stood firm. And, Paul, bless his heart, kept coming back and trying until it was just indisputable that he was the perfect person for the role."

Agents need no convincing to get their clients to do Disney animated features. "There are so many things that make it a great opportunity," she says. "For one thing, we can work around actors' schedules. If you're working on a film in Florida, we'll record you in Florida. One of the directors of *Tarzan* recorded Nigel Hawthorne delivering his lines in Paris. They brought him over from London where he lives. If an actress is pregnant, it's no problem. If an actor doesn't sing, we'll find a singer for the vocals. When Demi Moore was playing Esmeralda it took some time, but we found Heidi Mollenhauer, a singing waitress at Don't Tell Mama, a cabaret in New York. She was the perfect vocal match for Demi."

Her advice to actors eager to break into animated film: "Study acting. Get creative."

Casting Disney animation "is the greatest," she repeats, "because there's no shame in our product. People enjoy working with us. I do, too. It's the best."

John Levey

WARNER BROTHERS TELEVISION

300 Television Plaza, Bldg. 140 #138
Burbank, CA 91505
(818) 954-4080
FAX (818) 954-7678

Many of the diverse actors appearing on the series *E.R.* every week have been the discoveries of John Levey, vice president of casting for Warner Brothers Television. Levey likes actors, and he's known to have given many their first roles. "Upstairs, here at the casting administration," he explains, "they sometimes call me John 'Taft-Hartley' Levey." That's because he often takes advantage of the Taft-Hartley Act to hire nonunion talent, first-timers he discovers in his extensive file of pictures and résumés, in local theater, and from his dealings in the community. Prior to *E.R.*, Levey worked on *China Beach*, which was cast with young people in their late teens and early twenties, and Levey couldn't always rely on established actors. Many minority actors, including Vietnamese, were needed for the show; and Levey's working relationship with the Vietnamese community in Los Angeles assisted him in his talent search.

Levey not only hires minorities for minority roles, but he enjoys casting women, "ethnics," and the disabled in parts not necessarily written for them. He prides himself on being more than a list-maker: "I hate the concept of type," he says. "I try to find a *human being* who embodies the qualities that the scene and the character require, and I try to go as far in it as the material will let me." He cites as an example his casting of Dana Delaney as Colleen McMurphy in *China Beach*. "The character was written for a flaxen-haired Midwestern beauty, but Dana got the job because of her heart and her eyes. She certainly wasn't what anybody was looking for, but she was the first person I thought of."

CREDITS INCLUDE:
E.R.
China Beach
O'Hara
Head of the Class
The Witches of Eastwick

Levey conducts his casting sessions

110

in a fairly routine way. He expects actors to conduct themselves in a professional manner and to be on time and prepared. He does not expect them to have the material memorized—that's up to the actor, he says. He does expect actors to ask questions pertinent to the part, and he'll talk to them to uncover their personality and their sense of humor. "I play with them a little to see if they come back at me with anything. I might challenge them, or I might flirt, or whatever, to try to get a sense of who they are." Levey may also ask about their previous experience or training.

As for dress, Levey is pretty flexible. It's really not necessary to dress in a nurse's uniform to read for a nurse. On the other hand, he suggests that if you're playing a district attorney, it's probably not a good idea to come in a bathing suit. It's not what you wear that impresses Levey—it's that elusive attribute *charisma*. He recalls the time he and his associate, Patricia Noland, were looking for a love interest for Delaney, a demanding part that took weeks to cast. They had seen nearly seventy young men before Tom Sizemore was sent over by his manager. "I had been at a meeting, and when I came back he was leaning against Patricia's desk with a cigarette dangling from his mouth, sort of blowing the smoke in her face—which she hates, normally—and she was looking at him like he was the cat's meow." He wasn't handsome, he explains, "but he was using his sense of humor, his audaciousness, and his confidence to take control of the room, and I knew he had the qualities that we were looking for."

Levey believes acting is about accessibility, identification, and sexuality. For an audience to be able to feel what the actors are feeling, "it takes a kind of openness and also a kind of enthusiasm for being human. You've got to love people to represent them in stories," he adds. "And if you do, it comes through, even if you're playing horrible killers or people in conflict. If you can embrace and express the humanness of the person, then you're likely to be very exciting to watch."

If you want to reach John Levey, don't phone him. "I hate phone calls. I don't have time for them," he insists. If an actor has something professional to communicate, such as a current theatrical gig or a change of agent, he'd prefer a note. Will candy help? No way! "If I have a bribery point," he quips, "it's higher than a piece of candy!"

Heidi Levitt

HEIDI LEVITT CASTING

Associate: Monika Mikkelsen
1020 N. Cole Ave., 2nd floor
Los Angeles, CA 90038
(213) 467-7400
FAX (213) 467-6689

Heidi Levitt has become the casting director of choice for many Asian-themed films. She worked on *The Joy Luck Club* and other films for director Wayne Wang. That's probably because of the amount of time she devoted to finding the right cast for the Oliver Stone film *Heaven and Earth* in 1992 when she worked with colleagues Risa Bramon Garcia and Billy Hopkins. The film was about the war in Vietnam seen from a woman's perspective. "We had to find the woman the story was based on," she explains. "We also had to find her whole family, and there aren't that many Vietnamese actors in the unions." To find out what she had to look for in the actors, Levitt started the casting process by getting to know the real-life character as well as possible. "Then we solicited within the Vietnamese communities all over the country. We brought on assistants who spoke the language. We wrote press releases and had them translated. We did open calls. We saw thousands upon thousands of people. We went to every major Vietnamese center in the U.S."

They finally found their "star" at the University of California at Davis. "She was a premed student who'd come to an open call with her sister in San Jose. Her name was Hiep Thi Le. She'd never acted before, but she was a natural. I'm sure there were over two thousand people auditioning that day. But when I saw Hiep I just had the feeling she was the one." They didn't use a script, but instead did improvisations with the actors, many of whom didn't speak English. "It was pretty amazing, but there was a real spirit to the people

CREDITS INCLUDE:
The End of Violence
The Rock
Smoke
Natural Born Killers
Heaven & Earth
The Joy Luck Club

that we found. They'd just jump in and improvise; they're very lively and performance-oriented, even though it's not traditional to be an actor in that culture."

The Joy Luck Club was different. "The Chinese seemed to be more introverted about performing. We did some open calls in Queens, New York, which has a community of Mandarin-speaking people. But since the script was more complex, it required more training on the part of the actors, and it was a lot harder to cast. We cast a few nonactors who spoke Mandarin, but by and large we ended up with a cast of experienced actors who were pleased to finally get national exposure through this film."

It's helpful that Levitt has studied acting. While attending college in New York City, she did internships in theater. Her graduate training was at the American Film Institute, in Los Angeles. "I have a good memory," she admits. "I'll see an actor and remember the person. I'd go to the theater in New York all the time and knew who the good actors were. Casting was a natural for me."

But she didn't know it at the start. "I read an article in *Esquire* about Juliet Taylor, who casts Woody Allen's films. I thought it sounded like a neat job." Levitt was working at CBS News at the time and wanted to be a documentary producer. "The problem was, I didn't want to leave New York and knew I had to go to a small town to get started." So she worked as a publicist for a while, until she read another article on casting, this one about Risa Bramon and Billy Hopkins, who had just done *Desperately Seeking Susan*. "I thought it was really great," she recalls. "I knew I couldn't get to the director, so I decided to write to Risa and Billy and see if I could get in as an apprentice." As a result of their meeting, she was offered a job, which she began after doing a stint as a director's assistant at Warner Brothers.

Levitt loved being able to find actors from the New York stage. "There were all these people working off-Broadway who hadn't gotten into film yet, like Kevin Bacon and John Malkovich—a great talent pool to draw from. I really learned a lot from working with Risa and Billy."

In Los Angeles, she observes, she has less good theater from which to draw. "The business has changed, too," she adds. "Actors used to graduate from drama school and go to New York or Chicago to get their feet wet in the theater. Now they come straight to L.A. and dive into film and television."

Levitt feels actors are doing themselves an injustice by not doing regional theater. "A lot of people who come here are simply not ready. It's too big a pool out here. It's hard to stick out in a crowd without building up experience." Today, Levitt's talent pool includes theater, film, TV, and agent referrals.

Levitt rarely has time for general interviews and prefers having actors come in to read for something specific. She'll chat briefly with them to find out a little about their background and personality. "I'm always looking for someone who is slightly different. After a while, people start to seem the same. I want to find an actor who's to the left or right of the norm." For example, she cites the casting she did for Oliver Stone on *JFK*: "When Tommy Lee Jones played Clay Shaw, it was an interesting leap. It relaunched his career," she says. "He was playing a sort of out-there gay character. Even Kevin Bacon was playing an unusual character." Levitt was proud of the casting of that film, for which she, Bramon Garcia, and Hopkins were responsible from the beginning. "When it's a big studio film, the producers will put in the stars before it even comes to the casting director. But when you're doing a movie with a director you've had a relationship with, you're probably in at the beginning," she explains. That's the relationship she has with director Wim Wenders, for whom she cast *The End of Islands*. "You have to be in sync as a casting director. Someone is buying your taste. If you're not in sync, you shouldn't be working together."

If Levitt believes in a certain actor for a role, she doesn't usually back down. "I cast *The Chinese Box* in Hong Kong for Wayne Wang. We didn't have a script, just the bare bones. Even then, I knew Ruben Blades would be interesting for the role of Jeremy Irons' best friend. Wayne liked the idea at first, but after a while he had second thoughts. I knew Blades could handle the role, which required an actor who could be open to improvising, and I fought for him. He got the role, and he is one of the strongest parts of the movie."

Levitt advises actors to be sincerely committed to their craft. "It doesn't happen right away, and you need to be in it for the long run. You have to realize you're going to be putting yourself through a lot of rejection. If you can go out there and do the best job you can, whether or not you get the job, then you have a chance of succeeding."

Meg Liberman

LIBERMAN/HIRSCHFELD CASTING

Partner: Marc Hirschfeld
4311 Wilshire Blvd. #606
Los Angeles, CA 90010
(213) 525-1381
FAX (213) 525-0131

Although she was already an established casting director, Meg Liberman decided about ten years ago to learn more about the people with whom she's in contact on a daily basis. She enrolled in a two-year acting program with Joanne Barron, a proponent of the Sanford Meisner Technique.

"I went to class every Monday and Saturday night for two years, and it was one of the best moves I've ever made in my career," Liberman attests. "If you're working with actors, you have to know how to approach them. One day I was interviewing a young man prior to his audition to get a sense of who he was, but after our talk, he'd basically lost his entire preparation for the scene. I realized then that I didn't have a clue as to why he found it difficult to get back into character and perhaps I'd better take a class."

Liberman believes every actor would benefit from the Meisner Technique, although she believes it's not the best system for auditioning: "It's not result-oriented. Auditioning needs quick-performance and cold-reading techniques." She recommends a study of both these and the Meisner Technique.

The first thing Liberman looks at on the résumé is training. "For me to have a dialogue with actors, I need to know with whom they've worked and how they've paved the way for a career." The next item of importance is theater experience. Film and television credits are last on the list. If you have had good training and you have a certain spark, you're sure to get Liberman's attention.

Being a product of a show business family, this casting director certainly has a knack for

CREDITS INCLUDE:
The X-Files Feature
From the Earth to the Moon
Seinfeld
Party of Five
The Days and Nights of Molly Dodd
The Wonder Years
Fame Series

talent. Her father was a press agent who had celebrity clients such as Bob Hope and William Shatner; her mother, Pat Harris, was a well-known casting director; her aunt Radie Harris was a columnist for *The Hollywood Reporter*; and her sister, Kay Liberman, works as a personal manager. "The most exciting thing for me, after all these years, is finding new talent," she explains. "Making those discoveries is the most rewarding part of the job. An actor will walk into the room and have that magic that distinguishes him or her even before reading. There's something indefinable that separates such people from the rest. They have a light inside them, a gift."

Discovering new faces during the casting of the TV series *Fame*, in 1983, Liberman had her first experience conducting nationwide talent searches for young people. At one open call, 5,000 actors showed up. "One of them was Jesse Borrego, but he failed to put down a number where we could reach him, and there was no way to contact him. We put an all points bulletin out on the radio to find him. Luckily, someone heard it and found him. He happened to be a student at California Institute of the Arts." Out of the 5,000, he was the only one she hired as a regular on the show. Don Cheadle was another Cal Arts student who showed up for the audition. While Cheadle was not cast as a series regular, he did get a guest shot, and he went on to do *Devil in a Blue Dress* and *Boogie Nights*.

Liberman doesn't feel it's necessary to peg actors as either dramatic or comedic performers. "I'm seeking good actors, and if you're really committed to the scene for which you're auditioning, it doesn't matter if it's comedy or drama. There are those actors who are comedically gifted," she adds, "but for the typical weekly show, if you completely believe in what you're playing and make a strong choice, you can do comedy." She doesn't feel that stand-up comics are always the best actors. She agrees that some comics with terrific personalities can have a successful show in which they star, so long as they have a strong ensemble cast around them. She cites Jerry Seinfeld as an example of a star who understands the importance of his supporting players. "When we did the pilot," she recalls, "we were casting at the network affiliates' convention at the Century Plaza Hotel. It was weird. I remember who tested against those who got it. Steve Vinovich tested for Kramer, and Larry Miller tested for the part of George. Jerry was really specific about whom he wanted, very involved with the selections, even though no one really had any idea where this show was headed. The first order was for only four episodes!"

Liberman was recently asked (for a book slated for publication following the final episode) which episode of *Seinfeld* was her favorite. "It was the one in which one of the characters was Meg, the casting director. She was portrayed as a fifty-year-old matronly lady, which didn't really bother me, and the funny thing is that the woman who played the part, Laura Waterbury, is now actually casting for the Pasadena Playhouse."

Another of Liberman's favorite shows is *Party of Five*, which she's been casting for several years. At times it's particularly rewarding: "Brenda Wehle, the grande dame of the Guthrie Theater, in Minneapolis, had just moved to Hollywood. She'd never done TV before, but one of our directors had worked with her at the Guthrie and cast her. There's no barrier in our quest for talent. Actors can be middle-aged or older. If they're talented, they can still be discovered."

Liberman/Hirschfeld has been one of the busiest casting firms in Los Angeles for the last eleven years. Between the two casting directors, they have accumulated ten awards from the Casting Society of America and have been close to an Emmy on several occasions. "Marc has been pushing for the Television Academy to separate the Emmy categories for comedy and drama, but they won't budge. We always lose out to shows like *E.R.* and *Chicago Hope*."

This casting team has managed to avoid what most others have not: to be type-cast in one medium. Liberman/Hirschfeld does film, series, pilots, miniseries, and theater. One of Liberman's proudest accomplishments was casting Eugene O'Neill's *The Iceman Cometh*, with Al Pacino, in a staged reading at the Garry Marshall Theater, in Los Angeles. "It was really difficult to get so many actors to commit to a long rehearsal schedule with no pay. We needed very specific characters, most middle-aged, and there were 250 pages of script!" But she pulled it together, and they're discussing the possibility of taking it to Broadway or doing the play on television.

And she is venturing into producing. "I've started with a wonderful relationship movie, *Dancing About Architecture*, which was picked up by Miramax. It's the hottest script in town." With *The X Files* feature and Tom Hanks' miniseries *From the Earth to the Moon* and her new producer credit added to her résumé, Liberman is happy in her work. "I love what I do, and if you're an actor who loves what you do, then be persistent. There are so many ups and downs, but ultimately it will pay off if you're great. You have to be great, because there are a million people out there who are just okay, and okay is simply not good enough!"

Valerie McCaffrey

NEW LINE CINEMA

825 N. San Vicente Blvd., 3rd floor
West Hollywood, CA 90069
(310) 967-6750
FAX (310)967-6701

Valerie McCaffrey has an extensive roster of film credits—so extensive it includes two films with a nearly identical title. While working for Universal, she helped cast the movie about Babe Ruth entitled *The Babe.* Later she had sole casting responsibilities for *Babe,* the Oscar-winning (for visual effects) movie about the endearing little pig.

Casting *American History X* was an intense experience. The script called for actors to portray skinheads, and, since it isn't the kind of look or attitude you find in the *Academy Players Directory,* McCaffrey had to open the casting to the community. "We had an open call, and I must say I'd never been in a situation where I was scared. There were actors with pretty strong opinions. I couldn't tell if what they were voicing were their real opinions or if they were acting—and some were pretty strong emotions. There was a fine line between reality and fiction."

In two open calls in Los Angeles and New York, they found one person they hired for the film—a lot of work to find one actor. Nonetheless, it's a rewarding job for McCaffrey. "My favorite part," she says, "is when I can actually give someone the job. I love finding new talent, when an actor comes in and blows the room away. That's the whole reason we're here. When they move you at an audition to the point of tears or joy, it's incredible."

What is less pleasant for McCaffrey is having to validate herself as a casting director. "People just don't know what we do. Some producers

CREDITS INCLUDE:
The Legend of the Pianist on the Ocean
American History X
Dark City
Money Talks
Mother Night
Babe
The Island of Dr. Moreau

don't even know what we have to go through to find an actor for a role. It's tough." Going to the theater and to every single movie to know who's out there "is a twenty-four-hour job."

Everybody knows what the actor does and what the director does, but casting directors are still fighting for membership in the Academy of Motion Picture Arts and Sciences and for Oscar status. People think because a lot of the time major stars are attached to projects, that's the whole story. There should be more recognition of "the difficulty of putting all the pieces together."

McCaffrey, whose title is Vice President of Feature Casting for New Line Cinema, received her B.A. in radio, television, and film, with an emphasis on theater, from California State University at Long Beach. She has also taught drama on the Universal Studios lot to kids in a gang prevention group, in conjunction with the Los Angeles Police Department. "Universal gave me a conference room to work in. I was a pretty tough teacher. At first, when I started, they were walking all over me. I was just trying to be nice. Then I thought, 'Okay, I can't play it this way.'" One youngster, she recalls, decided he didn't want to deliver a monologue she'd assigned in class. "So I told him to get out of the class and see his police officer. He said 'What?' I said, 'You heard me. I come here every week prepared. We're all waiting for you, and you're not prepared, so you're out.' Well, as soon as he saw the officer he came right back and said he was ready to do the monologue. He stood up and delivered it word for word."

McCaffrey is not easily intimidated. "If I don't think a certain actor would be right for a part, I'll try to convince the producers or director." She equates her negotiation skills with those of an attorney. "It's almost like you're building a case. You need to prove not that they're wrong, but that their choice may not be the best. We're supposed to be experts, and it wouldn't do a production any good if we went ahead and agreed with everything someone said when we knew one actor couldn't hold a candle to another. You have to be smart, but you also have to be diplomatic."

Diplomacy is part of an actor's responsibility, too. "Some actors just don't know how to take suggestions. I find that shocking. If an actor has that attitude with me, how is he or she going to be with the director?" She cites an instance during the casting of Giuseppe Tornatore's *The Legend of the Pianist on the Ocean*. "I gave the actor some suggestions. He had a chip on his shoulder instead of thanking me for the tips. Since the director wasn't in the room, I was his only voice of reason. He'd made a choice that wasn't the best, so I simply redirected him, and he was put off by it. He didn't get the job."

Another thing that actors do to limit their chances is set up "roadblocks." "They'll say, 'This role is not right for me. I'm too young or too old or not the right color.' They have no idea what direction we're going with the script. They've already dismissed themselves from the project. The point is, go in, do your best reading, and let the casting director decide if you're right for the role. Don't sabotage your chances. I can't tell you how many times that's happened."

Valerie McCaffrey feels fortunate to be in her position. "I've loved all the movies I've worked on. I'm drawn to good scripts just like actors are. And I love actors. I wouldn't be doing this job unless I loved actors." Her advice to actors young and not so young: "Just hang in there. You're never too old to get a break!"

Lisa Miller

LISA MILLER CASTING

1040 N. Las Palmas Ave., Bldg. 24
Los Angeles, CA 90038
(818) 954-7586
FAX (818) 954-6451

Lisa Miller equates her job with puzzle-solving: "It's all a giant puzzle, fitting the pieces together. As with puzzles, it can be frustrating." Having cast two seasons of *Fresh Prince of Bel-Air,* Miller recalls one episode: "I met a woman and fell in love with her talent. I brought her to the producers six or seven times. It got to be kind of a joke. When I'd bring her in, the producers would laugh and greet her like a long-time friend: 'Oh, Lisa's bringing her in again.' But I knew it was just a matter of time and finding the right thing for her. Well, she finally booked it the seventh time. It's that square-peg/round-hole syndrome. If you make an impression, I'll find the role you're right for."

Miller began her career in casting as an assistant to Peter Golden. Next, she paired with Cheryl Bayer. When Bayer took a job at ABC two and a half years later, Miller went out on her own. Lately, she has been working on the popular series *Everybody Loves Raymond.*

Her most exciting casting coup on that show was recruiting Peter Boyle for one of the leads. "I've been a Peter Boyle fan for years. Ever since I saw the episode of *The X Files* for which he won an Emmy. I couldn't stop talking about him."

Since the series is set on Long Island, New York, Miller is always on the lookout for the "New York Italian" type. "We need Boyle's poker buddies, the guys Ray plays ball with at the local high school, guys who work at the pizzeria, neighbors. . . ." (Valley girls need not apply!)

Unlike her previous show, *Space: Above and Beyond,* which had between twenty and thirty characters per episode, *Raymond* requires perhaps one

CREDITS INCLUDE:
Everybody Loves Raymond
Fresh Prince of Bel-Air
Pacific Palisades
Space: Above and Beyond

or two guest stars each week. But unknowns do have a shot, as they have on most of the pilots she casts. Miller keeps a series of notebooks in which she records every casting session she's ever had. "I know what I've written about everyone who comes in. I have this uncanny ability to remember people. I guess it's a muscle—if you exercise it every day, it develops."

Miller recalls a pilot she and Cheryl Bayer had just three weeks to cast. They were in readings day in, day out, with stacks of phone messages after each session. They couldn't possibly return every one. "One day," she recalls, "we finished very late and were making a list of whom to bring in when the phone rang. It was an agent who figured we'd been at readings all day—could he help us? He proceeded to go down his client list, discussing each actor with us, some we knew and some we didn't. And one of those, whom we didn't know, we wound up casting for the pilot." That, she says, was an agent doing his job.

"It's great when you don't have the pressure of having to find a star. It's very frustrating when you take on a great script and you know the obstacle will be having to attach a name to get the network interested. I like pilots that are purely about me being in a room reading one hundred actors a day and finding some great new untapped talent."

What is Miller looking for? "The actor who comes in and makes you sit up in your seat," she explains, "who just brings great energy and thunder to a scene you've heard a million times."

That actor should be prepared "whether it's the guest lead or a one-liner," she advises. "Make a choice about who that character is. Show me things in the scene I hadn't found before. I want you to bring the best part of yourself to the show." She is especially awed by those who make a strong impression with a single line. "One-liners are the hardest for me to cast," she says. "If an actor can come in and say, 'Hi, here's your pizza,' and make me laugh or take notice, that's what I'm looking for."

What she's not looking for is the actor with disdain for television. "Rule number one: Understand the tone of the show you're auditioning for," she insists. "An actor needs to know the beats and the comedy and what they're going for. Is it real, sketchy, or cartoony? When actors tell me they don't watch TV, that's so condescending. That's what I'm casting, and if you're a working actor, at least 40 percent of what's open to you is TV!" She encourages actors to watch at least one episode of each show to become familiar with it.

She also insists on a professional demeanor from an actor. "I behave in a businesslike manner, and I expect actors to respond in a similar way."

Miller tries to get to the theater at least two or three times a month, and she's adamant that actors keep their muscles flexed in classes and in live performance. "What's important," she adds, "is finding a teacher who's going to work on the things you want to work on. It's all very subjective, so you have to try to audit the class if possible, be it scene study, commercials, or improv. I always want to know with whom an actor is studying."

Lisa Miller loves it when a struggling actor finds success. "I just attended a one-man show, and it was a packed house for the first time since the actor put his routine together. It was great to see, because I know this is something he's been working on for months, and the response had been pretty weak. But he was persistent, pursuing people, sending flyers and calling everyone to remind them of the date. He's someone I like and whom I've read several times. He stuck with it and didn't give up despite the obstacles." She says she can't wait to witness another such "happy ending."

"Actors are the bravest people on the planet and have my utmost respect. All I'm asking for is that they, in turn, display the same consideration."

Rick Millikan

RICK MILLIKAN CASTING

Associate: Stacy Wise
Twentieth Century Fox
10201 W. Pico Blvd., Bldg. 75
Los Angeles, CA 90035
(310) 369-2772
FAX (310) 369-2284

If you're a fan of *The X-Files,* you may know the name Rick Millikan, who has been casting the cult favorite since its inception; his name is prominently displayed in each week's credits. In fact, he often feels like a celebrity in restaurants and stores when clerks and waiters recognize his name on his credit card. Or at parties, he'll be just "another guy" until someone mentions his name, and it's all over. "They hear my name, and it's 'Oh, I love the show. I want to do it so bad!' Then it becomes a whole drama, and I have to deal with it." He admits, however, he's flattered and very proud to be part of the mystique.

Millikan started casting television around 1987 as an assistant to Marc Schwartz, now a prominent agent. He helped Marc cast *Dynasty,* a popular series at the time. He's now working as an independent.

It's just as difficult for a casting director to make the transition from television to film as it is for an actor, he attests: "It doesn't make sense. We're all after the same talent, really. It's just a matter of whom you have access to, who's going to be interested in doing your projects. In feature film, you sort of have the bag open to everybody. In television, the bag is a little tighter. You don't get the pick of everything, and when you do, you always try to go for the biggest you can get."

In casting for TV, Milliken works with different types of material, "so naturally I'm looking for different types

CREDITS INCLUDE:
The X-Files Series
Sabrina, the Teenage Witch
Married...with Children
Kindred Pilot
Bedtime Showtime

of people. *Sabrina, the Teenage Witch* is more of a family show, a kids' fantasy, whereas *The X-Files* is a much more realistic show. I probably bring in more people for *The X-Files,* since we use off-the-wall characters and need a bigger selection to choose from." He admits he's far from the only person involved in the selection. "It's not just me sitting there making the decision. That'd be too easy. You've got to please the producers. Television is pretty much a producer's medium. They have the final say. Ultimately they're the ones writing the show and know exactly what they want. I'm not the boss. I'm just here to deliver the goods."

Some of those Millikan brings in are actors he's found in the theater. He'll see a show if he hears it's worthwhile, either in Los Angeles or New York. "We have a person at Fox in New York who videotapes auditions for me. I've had New York actors' tapes sent to me here for certain roles. All it takes is a phone call." Of course, he realizes there are some stage actors who can't quite adjust to the intimacy of film or television. "Especially newcomers, who don't realize that less is more. That the microphone is three inches above their head, and the camera is right there. There's a technique that has to be developed." Harriet Harris is an example of an actress who knew how to make that transition. "I had just gone to see *Jeffrey* at the Westwood Playhouse. I'd finished reading the next episode of *The X-Files,* and I was looking to fill one part in particular. When I saw Harriet, I knew she'd be perfect, and I brought her in the next day." She booked it, as he knew she would.

Rarely does Millikan attend a casting workshop, although his associate, Stacy Wise, does. "We've used quite a few actors she's met for *Sabrina* and *Married . . . with Children.* We always need day players, and the workshops are a good source for that." *X-Files* is more difficult to cast through workshops. "The caliber of actor is very specific," he explains. "We need very experienced people. That's not to say it can't happen, but it doesn't very often." However, he encourages actors to attend workshops to meet casting directors and get the experience of reading sides from actual television shows.

Millikan also encourages actors just starting out to find a small or midsize agency for representation. "The top five agencies deal with stars," he says. "I wouldn't suggest going to the top, because you'll just get lost. You'll only get mixed in the shuffle with Schwarzenegger and DeNiro. You want to get into an agency where they'll pay attention to you, where they know who you are and what you can do, not wind up in a file shoved into a drawer and ignored."

When you are sent out, the most important thing to Millikan is your professional attitude. "I want to see an actor who is courteous, who doesn't take too much of my time, is ready to go, and gets right down to work. If I want more, I'll ask for more." What he doesn't want to hear is "When is the callback?" "It puts me on the spot," he says. "I may not know whether I'm going to bring someone back, so it's an awkward situation"—not what a casting director wants to encounter. "I had an actor audition for *Sabrina*; it was for the part of a guy who's being interviewed for a date. The actor came in with a towel around his waist, and he turned around at the end and mooned the producers! He thought it was funny. It wasn't. It was completely embarrassing!" In other words, it was unprofessional.

Millikan feels an actor has the right to ask questions at an audition, but not merely in order to make an impression. "I can tell the difference," he warns. "I know a stupid question when I hear one, if it's already written in the sides or is pretty obvious." And if there's time, it's fine with Millikan if you want to stop and start again. "If we're running behind, we'll tell you, but there's no penalty for asking. What I don't want to see is an actor starting from the top and doing it exactly the way he or she did it before, because the producers will feel it's the only way the actor can read the scene and that's what they'll see on the set. If you're going to redo the scene, it had better be different, an improvement." At a callback, Milliken he expects actors to interpret the scene the same way they did at the audition, unless he asks for a change. "Generally, the reason we bring actors back is because we liked what they did the first time."

Rick Milliken enjoys reading with actors. He did a little acting himself after college. "I realized it wasn't going to be my end-all career, so I pulled out. I didn't like the idea of making fifteen hundred a year." Reading with actors keeps him in practice and tells him how the actors are responding to the material. "I just love to get into the scene with them," he chuckles. "I'm really getting good at Mulder and Scully."

Bob Morones

BOB MORONES CASTING

San Mar Studios
861 Seward St.
Hollywood, CA 90038
(213) 465-8110
FAX (213) 465-1874

Most likely, an actor will meet Bob Morones only when he's casting a project the actor may be suited for. He tries to avoid general interviews or auditions. "I would much prefer seeing someone do a scene in an acting workshop, on the screen, or on video," he explains. The only favor he asks is that actors please pick up their videotapes after a month or so. "I must have about five hundred of them sitting here, some that've been here three or four years—from major stars, too."

What Morones wants to see in an actor is pure, unadulterated talent, whether it's natural or developed. "If you can transport us into your world and into the character of that world, then you've done your job. Make us forget about everything, give us a new sense of time and really play on our emotions." One such actor who had a riveting effect on Morones, during his days at Universal Television, was Nick Nolte, whom he spotted in a performance at the Contempo Theater. "I tried to get the producers of *Rich Man, Poor Man* to bring him in for a reading, but nobody knew who he was, so they refused." But Morones believed in Nolte and insisted that the director see his performance. He did, and Nolte got the job. "That series launched his career and showed the world that he was an excellent actor."

To Morones the number-one thing that can ruin a potentially good performance is nerves. At auditions he sees actors destroy their chances by failing to overcome the jitters. "Actors get uptight, the words don't flow properly, and their timing is off, usually because they're not confident. They've stopped training or working out."

CREDITS INCLUDE:
187
American Me
Salvador
Platoon
Pumpkinhead
Storytime PBS

Training is vital: "Training gives you confidence, and once you have that, you can release the restraints you put upon yourself and be honest to the character you're portraying. People believe an honest performance. If they see you *acting*, they're put off."

Training alone isn't the answer, however. Acting also involves a combination of honing your craft and living life—"being an *observer* of life. That's an education. And the more educated you are, the easier it's going to be to grasp things and see things others wouldn't. Because what happens is that you can become prejudiced and closed to the richness of other cultures and ideas. Education opens you up."

Morones is known for his color blindness when it comes to casting. For the Kevin Reynolds film *187* with Samuel Jackson, Morones was asked to "give the picture a more American overview" and to find strong actors with ethnic identities who would present an accurate picture of America in 1988. "One challenge was that there were so many stereotypes that I had to find actors who could balance the film out or do strong portrayals that would counteract negative stereotypes." And balance it he did. He brought in many talented young people. "A lot of the kids I knew since they were children," he recalls. Morones had covered the Inner City Cultural Center often in the past; there children from low-income areas had the opportunity to perform. "I used to go there and watch plays, and a lot of the actors who came in to read for me, or whom I'd see in commercials, I remembered from those days."

One of the kids was Clifton Gonzales. "I remembered he had changed his name, and he did a wonderful audition. He must have come in eight times through the screening process, getting stronger and stronger in the character, and he wound up becoming the lead."

It was much the same process for Oliver Stone's *Platoon.* "We kept bringing actors back ten, twenty times to assemble a strong core group. A platoon or a gang—it's the same thing: you need strong camaraderie. Stone, like Reynolds, wanted chemistry among the performers to tell the story, focusing on the dynamic levels of each character. If the director has a real vision or passion don't be surprised if he brings you in time and again. He just wants to find the best combination of actors to accomplish his goals. Some actors get ticked off, but the ones who hang in there are the ones it pays off for."

Morones recalls a *Platoon* anecdote: One actor who helped Morones read other actors at auditions was Charlie Sheen. Morones felt that Charlie would be terrific in the film, "but Oliver didn't even want to meet him. I guess he'd met him before and didn't feel he was right for this project. I knew he'd grown as an actor, so I showed Oliver a clip of another young actor that also featured Charlie. Oliver was sure the other actor was Charlie's brother, Emilio, and I asked him if he thought we should bring the kid in. He said, 'You know Emilio isn't available.' When I told him it was Charlie, he was stunned." Of course, Stone used Charlie Sheen in *Platoon* and cast him in *Wall Street*, as well.

"One thing I've concluded as a twenty-five-year veteran of casting," Morones says, "is that the fastest way for an actor to lose the callback is to be unprepared, to think of this as a cold reading." Unlike many casting directors, Morones recommends an actor memorize the material prior to the audition, especially one for a producer or director. "It's extremely important for the actor to be prepared. Even though it is a 'cold reading,' it should not be." He knows being off-book is demanding, "but this is a demanding industry. The more off-book you are, the more you're prepared. I don't care if you forget the lines, I want the essence of the character."

He gets upset when an actor shows up fifteen minutes before the reading to look at the sides. "Even though the actor may be very talented, he's leaving the director with a bad impression. There's no excuse today for an actor not to get the sides from Showfax [the company that faxes material to actors at home] or from the casting office the day before the audition. No actor should come in and not be prepared to give a PERFORMANCE."

Morones frowns on the cold reading workshops that permeate the industry. "What's that about?" he asks. "What happened to performance? Are they doing a service or a disservice to performers? Throw them away! Why should we waste our time watching cold readings when we want to see an actor bring magic to the material?"

Morones advises actors aiming for the top to plot their careers wisely, "actually designing a career as if they were going to college, with checkmarks along the way, either quarterly or triannually. Actors should carefully budget their time. After four months, they should have accomplished so much, and after a year, so much. If they do that, by the time they get to the third year, they see themselves getting somewhere." Of course, Morones realizes it's not always easy to do it on one's own, and he suggests seeking a good manager or coach to ease the way. "You need a guide, be it a spiritual leader or even a grandmother, someone who's going to keep you honest. Because if you're not, the years are going to come and go, and nothing's going to happen."

Barry Moss

HUGHES MOSS CASTING

Associates: Julie Hughes, Jessica Gilburne, Ed Urban
1600 Broadway, Suite 703
New York, NY 10019
(212) 307-6690
FAX (212) 307-7179

The Hughes Moss philosophy is to maintain an open-door policy to actors. "Anybody can walk into our office and leave a picture and résumé," says Barry Moss. "We'll even try to talk to people when they come in, if we have the time. We're always looking for actors. We really feel that actors are a product, and to cut ourselves off from them is like cutting off our nose."

Moss never knows what talent may walk through his door. It's happened time and again. "We were casting a pilot," he recalls, "and in walks this guy who said he was perfect for it. We told him everybody in the room had an appointment, so he just waited. Three hours! Well, I was running around the office and kept seeing him sitting there, so finally I brought him in, and he got the part."

Moss always tells actors that if there's a role they think they're right for, stop at nothing to get it. Just be sure you're selective. "Don't just decide you're right for every role that comes along. Because after a while, if you're constantly persistent and obnoxious, a director will think that's the way you'll be on the job and won't want to hire you." But if an actor truly believes he's right for the role, Moss encourages perseverance. He remembers when he was looking for a dancer: "I saw a twenty-five-year-old Hispanic woman with a wonderful voice and fifteen years of dance experience. I asked her why she hadn't auditioned for *A Chorus Line*. She said, 'I sent a picture, but you didn't call me.' I said, 'That's a once-in-a-lifetime part, the part of Morales, and you would have been ideal. You

CREDITS INCLUDE:
Titanic
Jekyll & Hyde
The Will Rogers Follies
Crazy for You
Beavis & Butthead Do America
As the World Turns

should have been sleeping on my doorstep. You should have sent a carrier pigeon with your phone number; anything to get my attention!'"

Another thing that stands in the way of an actor getting a part is a lack of confidence. "They often come in with their heads slumped down instead of their chins held high. They're not there to help us with our job; they're there to be judged. Well, it's not about being judged. It's about coming in and solving our problem." That's why he feels there are so few actors who get the jobs, and the ones who do get them believe in themselves.

For actors who are unsure how to present themselves in the best possible light at an audition, Moss recommends Gordon Hunt's *How to Audition.* He believes it's the greatest aid actors can have, besides an understanding of their strengths and weaknesses. It's also imperative that actors read a script before an audition, and he suggests finding out as much as you can about a director for whom you're reading. "Talk to other actors who have worked with that director. Find out what the director has done before." And when you're into the audition, take your time. "If you feel things aren't going right, you can excuse yourself and ask to start again. Nine times out of ten, they'll say it's okay."

If an actor is auditioning for a musical, selecting the right song is very important. "What you should do is find an audition piece that fits your voice beautifully—just like a dress should fit you beautifully." He also stresses the importance of acting the material, not simply singing it. "You should be telling a story. It has lyrics, so think about what you're singing. Pretend you're singing to Rhett Butler. It doesn't matter, as long as you can put yourself in an acting frame and really communicate."

He also advises singers to stick with the material they have prepared. "Recently an actress came in for *Jekyll & Hyde,* and she said to the assembled group: 'The person ahead of me sang my song. Do you want to hear something else?' Of course they did, and she gave an ill-prepared audition." The point is that actors should not be worrying about competing with other performers, but should realize that they are unique talents, have something nobody else has, and therefore will do their song in their own special way. "Better to do an audition that someone else has done and do it well than to do something new and take a chance that it will bomb."

Because Moss casts a lot of theater, he's a stickler for training. "How can you do a job unless you've been trained for it?" he asks. He concedes that in film an actor can occasionally get away with little training, but he says it can never happen onstage or even in weekly television, where time is of the essence and professionalism a must. He advises actors to do scene study to keep their muscles flexed and to audit any class they're considering to see how they respond to the teacher. If the teacher believes in tearing apart an actor's psyche only to build it up again, it's harmful to the actor: "If you want your psyche ripped up, you should go to a qualified psychiatrist, not to an acting coach." He's adamant about this and cautions actors to be wary of certain teachers.

Moss is also frustrated with actors who profess to want to go to New York and do theater but, when the time comes and an out-of-town role is offered, make excuses. "They just want to sit around and wait for a TV show or movie. Their agents can't seem to multiply or they would understand that a steady income for a length of time can be more lucrative than a couple of days before a camera."

As for other words of wisdom, Moss encourages actors to simply do what they feel is necessary. "The casting director is on your side, kind of your little cheerleader." He likens himself to a sort of surrogate agent at times. "There's always someone you can count on. We'll remember someone from an audition two or three years ago and bring them in. So it's never over. Every time you audition, you put a little deposit in our safe deposit box of actors."

Meryl O'Loughlin

CBS TELEVISION

Associate: Gail Camacho
7800 Beverly Blvd. #3305
Los Angeles, CA 90036
(213) 852-2803
FAX (213) 653-0361

Meryl O'Loughlin has had a prestigious career in casting since the mid-1970s, when she was the executive in charge of talent at MTM Productions. Her responsibilities included supervising the casting of all the company's series, pilots, and made-for-TV movies. She was also responsible for developing new talent. Columbia TV hired O'Loughlin in 1981 as vice president of talent and casting. From there it was on to Imagine Films, in 1988, where she remained for three years. Her current position is with CBS, casting the perennial favorite *The Young & the Restless.*

Because of her experience working in talent development and conducting classes for actors in the art of auditioning, O'Loughlin is well equipped to hand out advice. The first thing she tells actors is the good news: There's a lot of work in Los Angeles. "The bad news," she says, "is that you can't do anything to experiment in front of a professional"—meaning that you must be really *ready* for the major leagues and you should not try to learn your craft in Hollywood. "If I were a young actor," she advises, "I'd get out of L.A. You can't go to Melrose Avenue and play a part you're wrong for just to learn, because you're going to be seen by professionals." Do your experiments, she suggests, in a small town or in New York, where there are hundreds of small theater groups from which to choose.

If you are a professional, a couple of pointers that she often reiterates to her students may come in handy. First, never memorize the script for an audition. "Never put that script down. Even if you have it memorized,

CREDITS INCLUDE:
The Young & the Restless
Aftershock—Tremors 2 Feature
Tad
Alf
The Mary Tyler Moore Show

never let me know, because if you put the script down, something more is expected of you; a much more professional, finished performance."

Second, avoid idle chatter. "Don't make jokes. Even if you know the people, don't start talking about your personal life unless they ask. Just do your work and get out." A thank-you is sufficient.

Third, dress to indicate the part, but never come in costume—that is O'Loughlin's preference. If you're reading for the role of a cowboy, boots and a lariat aren't necessary; on the other hand, if you show up in an Armani suit, she says, you probably won't get the role unless you're a star.

Fourth, O'Loughlin stresses the importance of being on time for an audition. If you happen to be early, don't sign in unless you're prepared to be seen right away. "The minute you sign in, they'll probably take you, because it's no longer what time your appointment is, it's who is there first."

Finally, one point that may not occur to many actors but is critical to O'Loughlin is what an actor says upon leaving an audition. "Never say to a casting director, 'Glad to have met you,' because you should never indicate that you don't know me. It's psychologically very bad for a producer and director to think we've never met." And never leave an audition, she cautions, until the next actor comes in. "What happens a lot of times is that you'll have given a good reading, but you weren't doing it *exactly* the way they wanted it, and by the time they say, "Gee, she was good, but maybe she could have done it this way,' and I say, "Well, why don't you direct her?" you've missed your chance if you've already left. So wait at least until the next person comes in. It can mean the difference between getting a job and not getting the job."

Study, study, study is the other key ingredient to being a successful actor. "Take dance classes, voice classes, movement classes, acting classes. That's where your money should go," she counsels. Before signing up for a class, however, audit it to make sure it meets your criteria. An actor should also invest in a couple of outfits for auditions, a decent 8 x 10 photo, and a professionally written résumé.

Although O'Loughlin discourages actors from sending in unsolicited videotapes, she does like to see an actor's work once he or she has read for her. "I love to see cassettes, because they're usually an actor's best work, stuff they've really, really done." For the casting of *Shattered Innocence,* about a young porno-film actress, she recalls, "It was a hard part to cast. She had to be beautiful, sexy, and a wonderful actress, because she was on every page of the script, starting out at seventeen and ending with her death at twenty-one. We saw many actresses. One had the looks, another the talent, but nobody had it all." Then she watched a videocassette that was on her desk, from an actress named Jona Lee. "It was so good! There was nothing on it but episodic television, but she had some good roles, and someone professional had obviously put the tape together. That's the beauty of having a well-edited, well-done tape."

If you're called in to read for O'Loughlin, be prepared for several callbacks if she's impressed with your audition. For a TV movie, there may be only one or two callbacks, but for pilots there may be three or four, since the networks are involved. She'll usually see thirty people a day when she's casting a television project, and time is of the essence. Her assistant will read with the actor while O'Loughlin listens and takes notes.

She shuns monologues, and although she realizes that cold readings are not the perfect way of determining talent, she feels they're the lesser of two evils. "Monologues are hard to do. You have to be very good to do one well." She's also concerned that an actor may have spent a year working on the monologue, which wouldn't show her how he or she could perform given a shorter rehearsal time.

O'Loughlin doesn't think talent alone is always responsible for success. "A lot of mediocre actors are more successful than some very good ones, because they're persistent and professional and don't get their feelings hurt. They keep plodding, and they make it. The bottom line," she says, "is to learn how to act and how to become a professional. They are two totally different skills. You can be a wonderful actor, but if you do not learn how to be a professional in Los Angeles, you will not work."

Johanna Ray

JOHANNA RAY CASTING

Partner: Elaine Huzzar
Associate: Mary Jane Lavacca
1022 Palm Ave. #2
W. Hollywood, CA 90069
(310) 652-2511
FAX (310) 652-4103

It's the essence of the person that is of primary concern to Johanna Ray, who is perhaps best known for her work with director David Lynch. She'll overlook a weakness in acting experience at times, if the person has a certain quality. She did so with both Wilt Chamberlain and Grace Jones. In the latter's case, she says, "I felt pretty sure she could pull it off, since there wasn't a tremendous amount of dialogue, and as for the physical specifications of the part, she fit them to a T." She cast Chamberlain in the same movie, *Conan the Destroyer*. As far as she knew, neither had any acting experience.

She would like to find the ideal combination of looks and talent, but it's not always possible. Working for Lynch, she believes, made her finely attuned to character. "David is the kind of director who will sit down and talk to a person and immediately tune in to certain qualities and be able to make them work. I've always said he could pick people off the street and get a performance out of them."

Having been an actress herself, Ray admires Lynch's knack for making actors feel comfortable. "He's very patient and painstaking, and he really directs actors, much more so than most directors." He's also quite open to suggestions Ray might present. When they were casting *Wild at Heart*, for instance, Ray wanted to bring in David Patrick Kelly, because she remembered meeting him for Lynch's film *Blue Velvet* and liked him a lot. "David ended up writing a part especially for Kelly because he was so intrigued by him."

Another example is with the cult favorite,

CREDITS INCLUDE:
Power of the Dog
Starship Troopers
The Player Pilot
Shakespeare's Sister
Lost Highway
Twin Peaks

Twin Peaks. They were searching for an actress to portray a role originally written for Isabella Rossellini. Ray suggested Joan Chen. Lynch again made script adjustments to hire her.

When Ray is working on a project such as *Starship Troopers,* for director Paul Verhoeven, she usually uses Breakdown Services and casts mostly from agents' submissions. "I know they are submitting, to the best of their ability, actors they think are right for a specific part. When actors send in their own pictures, they're sending them with the hope they'll be right for *something.* So basically, it takes up a lot of my time going through submissions that aren't even remotely close to what I'm looking for." She wishes actors could see the piles and piles of submissions she gets every week, most of which are unsolicited and not relevant to any project she's currently working on. Ray believes it's a waste of an actor's time and money to submit independently. "I'd encourage actors to work at a casting office or agent's office to see how many photos come in every day." (She herself worked for an agent prior to becoming a casting director.) "Then actors would understand how unrealistic it is to expect a casting call from an unsolicited photo. They'd also learn that rejection should never be taken personally. If an agent or casting director doesn't return your call, you'll understand. You've been there."

Ray doesn't like to do showcases in Los Angeles unless they're by invitation only and the casting director is one of the invited guests. She has traveled to Colorado to do a paid workshop with students in an acting school with which she was familiar. In fact, she found several actors that way whose pictures she keeps on file for future projects.

When Ray is meeting actors, she prefers they come in exactly as they are. The one thing that impresses her is not trying to impress her. "I like to make the meeting as social as possible, so that I'm getting the essence of the person. That way, when I bring people in to read, they make more of an impression as they show me how different they can be in character."

She has empathy for the shy actor who may not know how to conduct him- or herself in an interview, who mutters or is monosyllabic. "That's fine with me. It just says that the person is a shy, sensitive, and insecure person. It doesn't mean he or she can't act." She won't even take that into consideration when it comes to the type of role she'll have that actor read for. "A perfect example is Will Patton. When he came into my office, he was very shy and said he hated interviews. He'd much rather I see his work. His discomfort in the interview situation sort of endeared him to me." Patton had just taken over from Ed Harris in *Fool for Love,* in New York, where she travels often to scout for talent. The night Ray went to see him, she recalls, "He was electric!"

There are no absolutes in Ray's methods. Although she prefers that actors not use props at auditions, there are exceptions. When she was casting *Gaby: A Love Story,* Lawrence Monoson came in to read for the part of a cerebral palsy victim in a wheelchair. He'd researched the part to the point where everyone thought he was an actual patient. "He pulled it off, though it could have backfired. We saw a lot of actors for that part, but he was always the first choice."

Perhaps it's because, as Ray admits, she is a basically shy person who had to make a long, hard climb herself that she shows this sensitivity and flexible thinking. She was doing low-budget films for years until she was "discovered." To actors wanting to be "discovered," she offers encouragement to do as much acting as possible, no matter how unprestigious it may seem. "When you're first starting out, you may think this is not the kind of film you want to be in. But my advice is to take it, because that's just the kind of film you want to make your mistakes in."

Robi Reed-Humes

ROBI REED & ASSOCIATES

Associates: Andrea Reed, Cydney McCurdy, Doran Reed, Yolanda Hunt
8170 Beverly Blvd. #202
Los Angeles, CA 90048
(213) 653-6005
FAX (213) 653-6033

Robi Reed-Humes, who won an Emmy for the HBO film, *Tuskegee Airmen,* has been a casting director for about fifteen years, starting out in television as an assistant to Diane Demeo. Now she's casting both TV and film, and producing and managing—a Renaissance woman. She says the biggest difference between TV and film casting is the number of people who have a say in the final decision. "In television you have your network as well as your producers and director, whereas in film it's usually just you, the director, and the producer. You have a little more creative room with feature casting."

One of the few African-American casting directors in the business, Reed-Humes remarks on a recent improvement in job opportunities for minorities in film: "The projects have always been around, but now there seems to be an interest from the studios and networks. They realize there's a market for black films and television shows." She attributes much of the change in attitude to the success of such directors as Spike Lee, with whom she's worked since he appeared on the scene.

She also feels that black actors are getting more work because of their ability to hone their skills, something she says was difficult a few years ago. "By the time an opportunity opened up, you weren't as prepared. You need on-the-job training much more than just acting classes." Which is not to say that she's against an actor studying his or her craft.

Reed-Humes is a fan of the theater. The mother of two kids, she sees

CREDITS INCLUDE:
Sparks
Good News (also co-producer)
Clockers
Love Jones
Soul Food
Malcolm X
Do the Right Thing

fewer plays than she used to, but she's more impressed with actors who have done theater. Many of the actors Reed-Humes has hired have extensive theater credits and little film work. She advises those actors to take on-camera classes. "It helps, because the stage is bigger than life. I've noticed that on film theater actors seem too large and over the top, and it's simply because they're used to doing it that way for the stage. I wouldn't spend a great deal of money on classes—just enough to get the idea of bringing it down and containing it."

Open to actors with little or no on-camera experience, Reed-Humes pulled Kimberly Elise's picture from a stack of pictures sitting on her desk and auditioned her five times for a lead role in *Set It Off*, for New Line Cinema, "She looked interesting. She had just been signed by an agent, and didn't even have a SAG card. The studio was holding out for a name, but no one could deny her talent, and a week or two before filming she was hired."

Your picture is "your calling card," she explains. "Actors try to save money, but they have to think about the headshot as an investment in their career, their livelihood. A bad picture can prevent you from getting a job." It's a matter of getting what you pay for, she says. And as a manager as well as a casting director, she understands the impact of pictures. "I send my clients to photographer Robert Zuckerman, who uses natural light when he shoots. He manages to get the best out of actors, be they black or white, and provides lots of choices for me, which is difficult."

A neat résumé, carefully and accurately typed, is another requisite for an actor, as is a personal note to the casting director. Some actors may think a form letter with the casting director's name penciled in suffices, but she doesn't agree. "It takes only a couple of minutes, and it's so much more personal." Not only does it refresh the casting director's memory, but it's polite.

One thing Reed-Humes suggests actors *not* do is telephone her. "Calling on the phone and leaving messages for me to call back is ridiculous. A simple note saying 'Hi'—just to keep in touch or keep me abreast of what you're doing—is much more appropriate." She recalls an irksome situation when an actor tracked down Reed-Humes's home number and called her after-hours, and another when an actor found out which car she was driving and kept leaving pictures on her windshield. "When I did *School Daze*, someone even showed up at my mother's house!" She was not amused.

Reed-Humes is a firm believer in showcases. For her and her associates, workshops are a source of new faces. "A lot of agents also go to showcases. In half-hour television, we go through so many actors it's important to meet new people all the time for co-star and featured roles." She also believes in cold reading classes for all actors, "because that's what you're called on to do most of the time." If an actor gets good enough at cold readings, it's likely he or she won't even need a callback, unless it's for the director and producers.

Reed-Humes also tells actors that if they think they can improve on their reading at the audition, she'll gladly give them a second chance. "I don't say 'Okay, thanks. Goodbye,' after one shot. I think that's rude, and actors are subject to enough rejection. I try not to add to it. I think I still have a heart."

Shirley Rich

SHIRLEY RICH, INC.

200 E. 66th St. #1202
New York, NY 10021
(212) 688-9540

Shirley Rich began her casting career with Richard Rodgers and Oscar Hammerstein and has worked with other theater geniuses such as Harold Prince and Michael Bennett. To Rich, the most important thing on an actor's résumé is training. "I believe in studying. I feel you can study all your life. Any education an actor has, whether it's in psychology or drama, I want to know about it. I want to know how you learned to be who you are."

She emphasizes that an actor should *continue* to study: "Can you imagine walking onto a stage without having done a workshop or taken a class for a year?" She also encourages actors to find a survival job that allows a career. "You have to have another profession, whether it be in a restaurant or building cabinets. You must pay your rent."

When Rich calls actors in, they audition by reading from the script she has been hired to cast. "I've never done readings except for the thing I'm working on," she explains. "I guess it's because I'm theater-trained. I need to see an actor actually perform, either on the stage or on-screen, not in my office." And she goes to showcases a great deal to find good talent. "Theater training is the secret to acting, even though you may switch to another medium. If you look at all the actors today who have become names—DeNiro, Hoffman, Duvall, Hackman, and Streep—they were all theater-trained, and it shows in the technique and diversity of their talent."

Rich also feels strongly about preparation. She'll always provide as much material to an actor before a reading as possible. "I have never had actors read cold—maybe lukewarm, but never cold. If I cannot get the material to them ahead of time,

CREDITS INCLUDE:
Andre's Mother PBS
Taps
Kramer vs. Kramer
Saturday Night Fever
Crimes of the Heart
Theater

they at least must have time to look at it earlier that day." She'll also sit down and explain everything leading up to what they're doing. "They cannot," she adds, "do justice to the script when they have a mere two pages of dialogue. They can't possibly know the character's history and what's going to follow. It must be explained."

Unlike many casting directors, who simply don't have the time, Rich makes sure all actors who have read for her are notified as to whether they've gotten the role. "I feel strongly about that. It's the worst business in the world, right? What you've got to do, at least, is give them the chance to forget it and move on. And if an agent calls, I'll give any input I've gotten from the director to pass on to the actor. I'll tell them what I felt happened at the audition, because if it's something constructive, it can only help."

Rich's favorite moments come when actors surprise her with their talent and charisma. While casting *Taps,* she was looking for an actor to play Tim Hutton's roommate, an upper-middle-class sophisticated type. "In comes a kid that you would have thought had come out of Oklahoma's Dust Bowl," Rich recalls. "Gorgeous Sean Penn was not, sophisticated he was not. But he did a reading for me that was one of the most inspiring I've ever heard!" Rich rushed him into the producer's office and did her utmost to convince them of his ability. He got the part. "Sean Penn is really a brilliant character actor. He was only eighteen at the time."

One of Rich's more recent thrills was helping Edward Norton get a jump start with *Primal Fear.* Norton, like Penn, is an actor who can display a range. "Someone does a reading and *explores* it, maybe providing something no one else saw when reading for the part. If the director is secure, he or she is going to see it, too, and give that actor an opportunity to explore the part."

Rich tries to convince actors of the importance of making choices. "You cannot decide what all the people in that room have in their heads; you simply have to make a decision and go with it, sink or swim." An actor should also remember to take time with the material, she advises. "Don't rush. Take a deep breath, and don't start until you're ready." She also suggests keeping conversations brief. "To talk just because you're nervous doesn't benefit you." And avoid carrying a chip on your shoulder. "If you don't like the way your career has gone, keep it to yourself."

A final piece of advice: Don't be afraid to ask the director questions about the interpretation prior to a reading. "Those two or three minutes may be your life for the next year or ten years. Better make the most of it."

David Rubin

DAVID RUBIN & ASSOCIATES

Associate: Ronna Kress
8721 Sunset Blvd. #208
West Hollywood, CA 90069
(310) 652-4441
FAX (310) 652-4621

One of the attributes *The English Patient* had to offer was a splendid cast of characters. David Rubin was responsible for finding many of those individuals to appear in the Academy Award–winning film. He was impressed enough with Kristen Scott Thomas to schedule a screen test. But it wasn't just her acting ability. "It's important to get the tone of a piece right," Rubin explains. "Tonally, all pieces are very different from each other. I have to serve a script not only in terms of character but in terms of the time and place of the story. So when a period piece like *The English Patient* comes along, I look for actors who are credible in the period in which the story takes place. Kristen Scott Thomas reminds you of an old fashioned star. She has the style that fits the manner of the past. It's innate, it's the essence of that actor, and it's as important as his or her craft."

This blending of ability and look was equally important to Rubin when he was casting *Fried Green Tomatoes*. "I traveled a lot to the deep South for open calls in an effort to be accurate, so that when a Southern audience saw the film, they wouldn't be put off by uncharacteristic looks and sounds. Mary Louise Parker's look and energy seemed perfectly in place for the South of the 1930s." He's drawn to directors for whom accuracy is a priority: "It's one of the things that keeps me interested in my work. It's an opportunity to submerge myself in a culture that's entirely different from my own."

Before making the transition to independent casting, Rubin worked for

> CREDITS INCLUDE:
> *The English Patient*
> *Men in Black*
> *My Best Friend's Wedding*
> *Romeo & Juliet*
> *Fried Green Tomatoes*

Mary Goldberg, in New York, and Lynn Stalmaster, in Los Angeles. The training and experience he received were invaluable. He learned about collaboration in casting, the importance of understanding the director with whom you're involved. It's his belief that what the director expects of him is to suggest those actors who would illuminate the nuances of a role in unexpected ways. "This usually involves narrowing the thousands of possibilities to a very short list of varied but stimulating choices." In casting the housekeeper in *The War of the Roses,* for instance, many fine young comedic character actresses were passed over in favor of Marianne Sagebrecht, who, Rubin says, brought a cross-cultural twist and a unique sensibility to the role.

In smaller roles, he adds, the inclination is even greater to experiment with new faces or oblique approaches to casting. "The number of possibilities we can explore is usually limited only by time constraints and other casting priorities."

Rubin expects actors reading for him to have as complete a knowledge of the script, character, and production elements as possible, and be well enough prepared so they are connecting with the person with whom they're reading, instead of tied to the page. When the script is unavailable, actors should ask their agents or the casting assistant for information; and if details are still sketchy, they should make their own choices based on the material they do have. Rubin believes an actor need not memorize a scene for a first reading; most directors acknowledge that the audition process is exploratory in nature. Memorization is recommended, however, for a callback—and certainly for a screen test.

Before a reading, Rubin suggests asking questions about motivation, plot, and pronunciations. He may not answer them until after the reading if he wants to get a sense of an actor's instincts. He also recommends reacting to the reader as you would to another actor. "Your reactions are just as important as your own line readings." If you think you've blown the reading, don't jump to negative conclusions. Very often, Rubin says, "I can get more positive impressions from a botched but interesting attempt than from a slick, perfected one. I am entirely process-oriented in that regard."

Rubin is always looking for a variation on a theme, so to speak. In *Men Don't Leave,* writer-director Paul Brickman had written into the script an oddball neighbor with an unusual and inscrutable vocal pattern and world-view. "Some very fine actresses attempted to simulate the off-rhythms of Jody, but when Joan Cusack began to read, the clouds parted, the sun beamed down, and we had found someone whose unique comic timing perfectly matched and even enhanced Brickman's vision."

To Rubin, the difference between a fine actor and a movie star lies in an ineluctable quality, "a force of personality that a camera picks up, that engages an audience almost regardless of what the actor is doing on screen." Occasionally, he adds, one can get a sense of that luminous quality sitting in a room, but the only true test is from camera to screen. "I firmly believe that 95 percent of the time, a script is better served by the casting of fine actors than by the inclusion of one of the handful of 'stars'."

Because David Rubin is one of the busiest casting directors in Hollywood, he rarely has time to do general auditions with actors, even those he admires. "But I try to make clear to actors that, while they may not hear from me for years, when they do come in, chances are it's because they're right for the role, and odds are they'll land it."

Stanley Soble

MARK TAPER FORUM

601 W. Temple St.
Los Angeles, CA 90012
(213) 972-7374
FAX (213) 972-0746

Having cast a variety of television productions, Stanley Soble is acutely aware of the difference between camera and stage acting. Though there are many actors who can comfortably switch between the two media, there are others who can't. "Some actors have done so much television and film they've learned to act only for the camera, and when it comes to the stage they really have to work on their vocal skills to bring their voices back up to fill the house."

When Soble conducts auditions, they're usually in a rehearsal hall, a large room where actors must project to be heard. "We push the actors all the way to the back wall so they have to come out of themselves. They often get frightened by that. I've seen more than one actor who's been in television for a long time come back to do an audition for us, and they've lost the technique. On the other hand, there are those actors who make sure that every year, no matter where they are, they do some theater."

Actors who are used to doing film auditions and who find themselves in a rehearsal hall at the Mark Taper Forum may not be able to pull out of the intimate technique they've developed for film. "And we're looking for somebody who can use a technique designed especially for the stage to project the character, the voice, everything."

For that reason training for a stage actor is as important as training for a violinist or pianist, he says: "In film, good directors take enough shots so that in editing they can cover themselves. But in the theater an actor goes on and there's nothing to help him or her—no sound, no editing, nothing to save that person. Out there

CREDITS INCLUDE:
Angels in America
The Kentucky Cycle
Jelly's Last Jam
Lean on Me
Breaking Through
Miniseries

onstage, exposed, the actor has to deal with the situation. That's why technique is so important."

Actors at a typical audition are provided a chair. Other than that, it's up to them to choose how to handle the scene. "We just say the space is yours; do with it as you will. If actors want to move, they should feel free. When they're ready to start, they start. I try to make it as comfortable for them as possible. My feeling is that actors in to audition really feel they have no allies, especially when coming into a room where there's a producer, a director, the author, the casting director, and maybe even a designer. It's hard. They walk through that door and need to feel there's someone on their side."

Anyone who sends a photo and résumé to Soble gets seen by him; he looks through them all. If he finds an interesting face with some good training, it's likely that individual will be called in for a general audition. "I ask actors to prepare two contrasting monologues for me. If one is contemporary, the other should be classic. If one is funny, the other should be serious. The actor should try to show as many facets of his or her talent as possible."

He looks for *talent*—"an actor who is capable of coming in and not giving a finished performance, but giving enough of a performance that it will interest me, the director, and the producer. That's what we're looking for." The other thing he's looking for is *quality*. "People go through their lives acquiring a certain knowledge about themselves and the ability to reflect; that, in an audition, is what I call quality. We're all looking for that. People who can take the total of who they are and what they've learned and been through and project that through the reading—they are the much more interesting actors."

The first audition is usually just between Soble and the actor. The first callback will include the director. A third reading may include other actors in the cast. "We try to give actors at least a week's notice so they can get a copy of the script from their agents, take it home with them, read it, and work on the scene."

He doesn't expect an actor to memorize the scene; in fact, he's very opposed to that practice. He feels it's detrimental "because actors will often memorize the material, but they don't know how the actor reading with them is going to deliver the cues. It's far better to be familiar with the material but to keep the script in hand. It gives you a certain amount of security. You're not thinking about the next line." Of course, he expects actors to make eye contact and not be buried in the script, but he feels learning the lines should come after the actor has been given the role.

One of the ways an actor can get seen by Soble is to be a part of one of his many open calls; he conducts two a month. One is for Equity, the other for non-Equity players. About thirty actors are seen during each session. Equity auditions are preset; actors are asked to call ahead of time to schedule an appointment. The non-Equity calls are first come, first served, from 10 A.M. to noon. "We feel that it's important that the community has at least a chance to be seen without an agent."

Because he's working in Los Angeles, Soble realizes that not every actor will be amenable to reading for him. Film stars are used to being cast without auditioning for the role, and Soble finds it difficult to get some of them to agree to read for a play, even though their stage experience is limited. There are times, however, when star talent will read for the director. "When we were doing *Mystery of the Rose Bouquet*, we were interested in Jane Alexander and Anne Bancroft," he recalls. "Those two didn't have to read per se, but what we did is a reading of the play with them. After that, they made the decision whether or not they wanted to do it."

Soble spends as much time on the minor characters as he does with the stars. "You're putting together a group of actors, a chain that's only as strong as its weakest link. So we are as careful with the smaller roles as we are with the leading players." He's also responsible for casting the understudies. Most of those hired are not members of the primary cast, unless it's a repertory production or the cast is so huge that using a primary player is feasible. And sometimes an actor gets lucky. In one instance, they hired someone for a leading role who turned out to be so unsuitable they had to put the understudy in the lead just two weeks into rehearsal. At first, the producers had been reluctant to even hire the understudy actress, but they were delighted when she turned out to be much better than the person they originally hired for the lead.

Performing onstage is different in Los Angeles and New York. Soble thinks most actors who work on his and other L.A. stages are doing it for the exposure; they're on the West Coast to break into TV or film and hope they'll be discovered by casting directors who attend the theater to scout new faces. Does it bother him? Not at all. He's proud of the productions with which he's involved. "The important thing is that the well-rounded actor be aware of the particular field he or she is working in and learn to audition for each area in its own specific technical way. I really feel that unless you have a technique, a background, you're not what you call yourself, an actor."

Dawn Steinberg

BIG TICKET TV

Associate: Eileen Kennedy
1438 N. Gower St., Bldg. 35, Box 45
Los Angeles, CA 90028
(213) 860-7425

Y ou might think that the desk belonging to a head of casting would be less cluttered with headshots and the like than in-the-trenches casting directors working for her on specific projects. Not so. "The paper on my desk is unreal," says Dawn Steinberg, embroiled in the height of pilot season. "No matter how 'executive' casting directors are, we can never have a clean desk. There's just too much stuff."

Steinberg supervises casting for Big Ticket TV, which is part of Aaron Spelling Entertainment. She also does on-line casting for pilots. Among her credits are the pilots for *Moesha, Food and Company*, and the late-night syndicated comedy show *Nightstand*. "Being an executive as well as an on-line casting director keeps me in the trenches," she says. She has to stay current on who's hot in the pool of talent. "When we're in development, it's the most fun," she says. "I get to help package the pilots, marrying the talent with the writer."

Admittedly, the talent she's usually seeking are "brand names," but she provides hope to the generic contingent once a pilot is picked up by the network. "Once it's sold," she elaborates, "I can start seeing unknowns to round out the cast."

A casting director for fifteen years, Steinberg started out in New York doing the East Coast casting for West Coast–based casting veterans such as Fern Champion and Wally Nicita. Her last job before transferring to Los Angeles was director of daytime casting at CBS, where she also filled in on occasion for prime-time.

Like her Big Ticket gig, that was a staff job, something she'd previously shied away from: "I'm really picky about whom I choose to hang out with," she remarks. "I

CREDITS INCLUDE:
Moesha Pilot
Nightstand
Nightwatch
Pet Sematary

gravitate toward uplifting, happy people who want to be doing what they're doing. When I met the people at Big Ticket, there was instant rapport. It's nice to create your own department, setting the standard with the producers, writers, and actors."

Big Ticket casting has also brought its share of challenges. "*Nightstand* is the most unique show I've ever dealt with," Steinberg explains. "We cast thirty parts a week, and we look everywhere." Everywhere includes Breakdown Services, showcases, comedy clubs, and personal referrals. "If people tell me they know a funny actor, I tell them that person should call me, and I funnel the talent to Carol Barlow, who casts the show."

Nightstand is a great venue for new performers since it only pays scale and more established comics may not compete. "It's also great for established actors who haven't done much comedy and need to prove to their agents that they can handle it. They can come in and do it and get great tape."

Another source Steinberg consults are her notebooks. "Pilots don't usually give us much time for casting, so I usually go through agents and the notebooks I keep," she says. "Casting directors use notebooks for every project they've ever done. Before you do a project, you sweat the night before, putting dozens and dozens of names on lists, then checking their availability and interest prior to the pre-reading process."

Unlike many casting directors in town, Steinberg will set up a general meeting on the basis of an agent's suggestion or an interesting picture she's received in the mail. "I like generals," she says, "because during the audition process we don't really have time to get to know you a little. I can make notes in my book and go from there." She does several generals a day, as time permits. "I just want to get a sense of them, as people—see if they can make me laugh, see if I can make them laugh. I'm looking to see what's going to spark them and make them light up. Are they married? Do they have kids, a dog? It's like meeting someone in a coffee shop. We just chat."

Steinberg started guesting at showcases when *Nightstand* got under way. "I needed so many actors per week that I couldn't do that many generals in a day. If I went to these workshops, I'd see thirty people in one evening. We'd do scenes I'd brought along from the show and see if they could pick it up and do it. Then I'd add them to my list."

In New York, of course, the industry finds its actors in the theater. In Los Angeles, Steinberg confesses, it's tiring to travel to see theater in, say, Pasadena after a full day of work. "I'm just too beat.

I wish there were more plays here with bigger casts, so that when I go to the theater I could see a number of actors in an evening, rather than two or three. That's what's helpful about showcases."

Once she receives a script, she starts a lengthy process: She'll put out a breakdown and bring in actors for a pre-read. "I overcompensate," she admits. "I definitely have a lot of pre-reads when I'm casting a pilot. The number varies from role to role, but the producer may have a list of forty people to see. We'll narrow that down to twenty, knowing that twenty won't be available right off. Then I might want to throw ten unknowns into the mix." She may then do four days of pre-reads, a task she shares with her associate, Eileen Kennedy, whom she hired as her assistant because of her experience in theater and film casting in New York.

As for callbacks, that's the final step before taking the actors to the producers. Steinberg's choices are primarily well-trained actors. "Training is the most important thing under the sun: theater, voice, scene study," she insists. "I look for that on every single résumé." Acting classes are good for the actor also because "you do roles you wouldn't normally get. If you want to play an ingenue and know you'd never get the chance in the real world, take a class and do it. That's what you do in class, you play. It's like going to the gym. It makes you feel good about yourself."

Another training ground for young actors, she suggests, is daytime TV drama. "While some people thumb their noses at it, I think it's great training. It's a great way to make a living. You get great parts, and you can support your family."

The biggest pet peeve to Steinberg is physical contact. "Don't touch me. I'm serious," she warns. "All day long I meet actors. Someone's bound to have a cold or other virus, and it can spread. I tell actors I have a six-year-old I want to keep healthy. I prefer to say, 'Hi, how ya doin'?' and sit down." She especially dislikes physical contact during a scene. "I'm not an actor. Don't touch my face and tell me how much you love me. I'm not prepared for that."

For actors who are serious about their careers her advice is simple: Hang in there. "People say there are more actors than ever today. That's true, but look at the product. There are two more networks, there's TNT, cable movie networks. Everyone's doing original programming. There is, and will continue to be, a lot more opportunity for actors." Amen.

Mark Teschner

MARK TESCHNER CASTING

Associate: Gwen Hillier
ABC-TV
4151 Prospect Ave., Stage 54
Los Angeles, CA 90027
(310) 557-5542
FAX (310) 557-3150

Mark Teschner, who is the vice president of the Casting Society of America, won the Artios Award for outstanding achievement in daytime television casting. He may hold the record for casting the largest number of actors for an ongoing show: *General Hospital*. Daytime drama is one of the best vehicles for getting a start in TV, and because "GH" has one of the largest casts in that genre, it would behoove an actor to keep in contact with Teschner.

"I'm looking for any actor who's right for a particular role," he states, and if you're a nonunion player, it's not a problem. You can always join the union after you secure the part. "If an actor sends me a photo, and I want to read him or her for a role, I certainly will do so. Everybody has been nonunion at some point or other in their lives, and most have gotten their union cards by working."

There are usually thirty-five regulars on the show, and each year about six to eight actors are hired because of attrition. On top of that, ten to fifteen significant roles recur, and the day players, under-fives, and extras are always needed. Those who don't win the coveted roles may not lose out completely, Teschner says: "Many day players are cast from those who've read for larger roles. The way I see it, if 250 people have read for a contract role, and we can only hire one, there may be some terrific actors that deserve a shot at being on the show. It's a great source for discovering talent on a daily basis."

When working on *Loving*, Teschner recalls, he hired Terri Polo as a contract

CREDITS INCLUDE:
General Hospital
Port Charles
Loving
The Girl on a Swing
High Stakes

player. "It was her first audition. There was something very special about her despite her lack of credits. She had wonderful instincts." The producers created a part for Polo because they were so impressed with her ability—not an unusual practice in daytime television. Teschner says another part was created based on the discovery of unique talent a few years ago on *General Hospital*. Brad Lockerman, who acts a central role, had originally read for the part of Duke. "We didn't hire him for that," explains Teschner, "but we knew we wanted him on the show and envisioned something coming up in the not-too-distant future." So they kept tabs on him, and when they had a suitable role, he was hired.

The theater is another source of talent. "I go to the theater a lot," Teschner says. "One of my favorite things in casting is to see an actor in a show, make a call the next day, and offer him or her a part." Having come from a theatrical background himself, Teschner feels strongly that casting directors should take the time to see plays. "I'm so conditioned to going to the theater that if I just limited my familiarity with actors to videotape, I feel I wouldn't be doing my job.

"The casting process never stops," he explains, "because there are so many actors. There's no such thing as inactivity when you're casting daytime." After perusing the scripts and determining what roles need to be cast for the week, Teschner will speak to agents. Following the auditions, he'll decide whom to call back and what roles need additional searches.

There are often two callbacks with the producer. "Sometimes we change the audition scene in the callback process to show a side of the character that wasn't present in the first reading." A screen test is the final step, during which the actor is paired with the character on the show opposite whom he or she will play, a test of the dynamics and chemistry of the situation.

It's not necesssary, according to Teschner, that an actor know the story line as well as a fan might, but he does think it's wise to watch a few episodes and become familiar with the characters. Of course, if the role being cast is part of a new story line, it's less important; the producers themselves may not know exactly where they're going with the new character. "The bottom line," he explains, "is that an actor has to make choices in terms of what he or she is going for as that character, and what's going to happen or not happen, regardless of his or her familiarity with the show."

Why is it that everyone on daytime TV looks so perfect? "Daytime does have a tendency to hire very attractive people because it's about romance and our perceptions of romance and passion. But I think we're slowly getting away from that. Sexuality and beauty are things that often stem from within. That's the way it is in real life. If you look carefully, you'll see that there is a much greater range today than there ever was in the look of daytime TV. There are fewer plastic-looking people than there were ten or fifteen years ago—at least I hope so."

During his stint on *Loving*, Teschner, a firm believer in casting against type since he started in daytime, came across an actor who had a quality that appealed to him, though physically the man was wrong for the part. "Even his reading was a little unfocused, but he was so interesting and compelling that as soon as I dismissed him, I ran out to the elevator and asked him to come back and try again." Teschner worked on the scene with him and called the producer to explain the situation. "I asked the producer to please pay a lot of attention to him and give him the benefit of the doubt." That actor ended up getting the part. "He found a way to make the role work and made us rethink the role."

What Teschner doesn't like to see is a desperate actor. "When I talked to a panel of actors at a recent Screen Actors Guild forum, I told them not to speculate about what the casting director thought of them after an audition. There's absolutely no way to tell, and the actor who's worried about what we thought is not going to get the part. Those who get cast are those who audition, know they did as well as they could, and take that thought with them, realizing that regardless of the outcome, they succeeded."

He similarly advises actors not to try too hard. "Don't feel you have to sell youself. We want to see who you are, not what you think we're looking for." If an actor works too hard, he says, it can have the effect of "pulling" the character out of the scene. Another piece of advice: "Only act if you have to, not for fame or fortune. Ninety percent of union actors don't work. If during the periods you're not working, you still have the passion for what you do, continue." And remember, he adds, casting directors are on your side. "An actor should understand that we need actors as much as they need us, and perhaps if we look at the business in that way, there can be a healthier understanding of how we can work together to make it happen."

Joy Todd

JOY TODD CASTING CORP.

11811 W. Olympic Blvd. #105
Los Angeles, CA 90064
(310) 996-3127
FAX (310) 996-7732

Joy Todd, once an actress and stand-up comic herself, loves her occupation. "If it was up to me," she says, "I'd hire everyone who comes through my door." Unfortunately, she adds, that's not the way it works. "I try to look at a script as a tapestry, with each actor as a perfect stitch. When the tapestry is finished, it should be gorgeous. I do keep a large file of actors whose work I've seen or who've auditioned in the past, and I will often bring them back on another project."

Todd generally finds her actors by subscribing to Breakdown Services and going through an avalanche of agent/manager submissions. "Of course, I have a very good idea which agencies have superior actors, but I've learned that some of the smaller agencies often have surprisingly good talent." Having sat on the other side of the desk, she knows from first-hand experience that it's not always easy to get an agent with one of the better-known agencies. "But," she stresses, "a good casting director is short-changing herself if she sticks only to the top ten."

All casting directors are inundated with submissions and, as a result, can spend only a short time picking and choosing those who are to be seen. "We rarely have the luxury of poring over each and every photo that comes our way," she explains. "Working on *Joan of Arc*, we concentrated on actors who had classical training. Most of the callbacks were chosen from that group. The classics give actors a solid foundation—very much as dancers who study classical ballet receive a solid foundation for any other branch of that art form." And, she feels, casting should be done with an eye to ensemble, "with a feeling for reality in the relation of one part to another."

CREDITS INCLUDE:
An Intimate Gallery
Joan of Arc
Gettysburg Feature, miniseries
The Verdict
Homecoming
Fame Series

Sometimes Todd brings in actors just on the strength of their photos and résumés, which come through the transom. "The most fun is discovering exciting talent whose résumé doesn't reflect a whole lot of experience." Todd says she's gone searching the streets to find just the right talent. "I think my mother would have had a cardiac arrest if she saw some of the establishments where I've shopped for talent!" Sidney Lumet asked her on more than one occasion, "Joy, where did you find him/her?" Her answer was always the same: "Sidney, you don't want to know."

When time allows, Todd loves to teach. "I don't teach acting technique. I believe there are many people better qualified in the profession. But I think I'm a whiz at audition technique, which I incorporate into positive thinking. I know it works, because I have a zillion letters from students who have successfully used this process."

On some occasions she has had actors audition with contemporary monologues. "Sometimes a script is structured so that the dialogue is sporadic and doesn't give the talent anything to hang onto. *Prince of the City*," she recalls, "had over a hundred roles, and many of those parts were cast this way."

"Cream always rises to the top," Todd believes. "Not long ago I was working on a project that required a teenage girl to play the lead. To avoid problems with child labor laws, we sometimes cast those who are actually older but who can play younger. As fate would have it, a youngster of fifteen showed up and auditioned for me. Although she had very little experience, I flipped over her quality and asked her to come back the next day and work out the rough spots. She agreed, and at the end of the session I was sure I had found our star. I brought her in to see the director and producer, telling them how excited I was about her." Her audition was terrific, and they loved her. Did she get the part? "No. She didn't. It seems the labor law issue raised its ugly head once again, and after much soul-searching, the powers that be decided she was too young." And whatever happened to the girl? "I will gleefully tell you. Her name is Fiona Apple, one of the hottest new singers today. I couldn't resist sending the producer a copy of her latest full-page interview. Hooray, Fiona!"

Joy Todd doesn't expect actors in audition to give finished performances. "But I do expect you to be prepared and to stay focused." She reiterates her predisposition to actors: "If it was up to me, I'd hire everyone."

Susan Vash

PARAMOUNT STUDIOS

Associate: Emily DesHotel
5555 Melrose Ave.,
Von Sternberg Bldg., Room 101
Los Angeles, CA 90038
(213) 956-8377

From piano teacher to casting director—that's the career track of Susan Vash, who really wasn't sure what she wanted to do when she started out. "I couldn't get music students when I moved from Los Angeles to San Francisco, so I worked as a photographer's assistant and then as an assistant to a top theatrical agent, where I learned a lot about the business and realized it's where I belonged." It was frustrating, however, since all the good talent that signed with the agency eventually moved to Los Angeles where the work was. "I remember Peter Coyote wandered in one day and wanted to be an actor. We got him his first part, but once he started working, he left for L.A." The same thing happened with Kathy Baker, Fred Ward and dozens more.

In 1982 Vash returned to where the proverbial action was. "I wouldn't let MTM alone until I could get an interview with someone at that studio, which was one of the hottest at the time." Her persistence paid off. Unfortunately, it was a thankless and uncreative job that she landed: typing stuntman contracts. "I did it for one season and decided I preferred writing. Everything my partner and I wrote was optioned, but that's as far as it got."

Then a friend at Breakdown Services offered to place her with several casting people as a temp. "One of those for whom I temped was Sharon Hyams, an independent. She was my mentor. I worked on *The Golden Girls* with her and became her associate. I realized that this was the field I really wanted. As an independent casting director you have freedom."

CREDITS INCLUDE:
Just You and Me Pilot
Mad About You
Spin City
George and Leo
Divorce: A Contemporary Western
The Unknown Cyclist

Vash's big break came in the late 1980s, when Chris Gorman at CBS had a pilot he was having trouble casting. "They couldn't find the lead, and I was this improv junkie. I probably knew more stand-up comics than anybody in town. Chris knew that and came to me. They needed a guy who could do impressions, as well as act, for *Just You and Me*."

Vash brought in Brad Garrett. He was hired, and she wound up casting the entire pilot. Unfortunately, it lasted only six episodes, but Vash was on her way.

Mad About You put her name on the map, and she was suddenly a busy independent doing episodic TV. "The challenge is casting without the luxury of a final script, because they're most concerned with getting the script just right, and they're always in rewrites. We often have to get actors in at the last moment or cast the day of the shoot. It can be stressful." The other challenge for Vash is finding people with comic timing. "The producers are looking for beautiful *and* funny actors, and the two don't always go together."

She meets a multitude of actors when casting a sitcom, since she's doing a new show every five days. The payoff comes when she finds a gem among them. "When I brought Lisa Kudrow in, as Paul Reiser's blind date on *Mad About You*, I'd seen her at The Groundlings [an improv theater]. Danny Jacobson and everybody thought she was so funny, so Danny brought her back as a different character in another episode. That rarely happens. She was so good as the ditzy waitress, Ursula, that *Friends* asked for permission to use the character as Phoebe's twin sister. Now she's famous."

Vash also does independent features and loves hiring actors with different sensibilities who are perhaps too "heavy" for sitcoms. But the process is the same. She'll bring in an actor to read a scene. "I don't chit-chat. I want to hear actors read. I like to hear their rhythm, their comic timing. My associate, Emily DesHotel, reads with the actors, so I can focus on the performance." She'll bring in a lot of choices for a pilot, but for a more substantial role she'll make lists and try to narrow them down. She also seeks variety, different ethnicities and ages. "I'll try to bring in what they think they want and several choices we think might be more interesting. Sometimes it works, sometimes it doesn't. It's always fun when producers are adamantly against an actor, but when we bring him or her in, they completely turn around. It happened on *Spin City*. I felt a certain actor was born to play one of the roles, and once he read for the producers, they were sold. That also makes the producers trust us more."

Vash bemoans the adversarial role that many actors put casting directors in: "We really are on their side, and we're thrilled to find new people and are willing to work with them if they need it to win the role. Sometimes an actor thinks having to come in for a pre-read is an insult, but it's not. We're giving actors our time to make it work out." Vash rarely has the time to attend workshops and showcases to find new talent, but Emily is often invited and has hired several actors that way.

If you're talented and professional, you'll get a shot. "But you have to keep studying," Vash stresses. "Do whatever works for you: classes, workshops—but be honest with yourself. I know too many actors who think they're leading men and women when they're not. They're the second bananas, the friends, but they won't accept that, and they're miserable. Why can't you say: 'I'll never be Michelle Pfeiffer, but I can be her best friend'? That's more realistic."

The biggest demon in an actor's life, says Susan Vash, is insecurity. "You're not going to be right for every part. That doesn't mean you're not good. You may be wonderful, but your look may be wrong for the part. Trust yourself. Know your limits. Know who you are.

"It's hard. There's lots of rejection. Learn not to take it personally, because it's not personal. Rejection is part of the job description. You have to let it roll off you and keep going."

Katy Wallin

KATY & COMPANY

Associate: Thom Klohm
1918 W. Magnolia Blvd. #206
Burbank, CA 91506
(818) 563-4121
FAX (818) 563-4318

When you hear the terms "cattle call" or "open call," you might imagine swarms of Hollywood hopefuls gathered together, 8 x 10s in hand, waiting at the stage door practicing their lines or nervously chatting among themselves. Well, Katy Wallin has a good deal of knowledge about that aspect of show business. She has staged a number of nationwide casting calls in the decade she's had her own business. She recalls the hundreds of young actresses vying for the lead in *Madonna: The Early Years* for Fox Television. That particular session was covered by major newspapers and entertainment shows. And then there was the notorious *Mighty Morphin Power Rangers*: When that show was in its heyday, Wallin says, "we needed specific ethnic and age requirements, as well as special skills the kids had to demonstrate. We had to see hundreds of youngsters at a time, and open calls were the only way to go."

Wallin, who has now branched out into producing with her company, Mystic Art Pictures, has cast more than 400 hours of network television. She works closely with agents and puts her calls out through Breakdown Services. She staged a worldwide search for the actor who will play Saul, in the biblical epic *The Emissary*, and she is constantly scouting talent for the kid's show *Beetleborgs*.

Kids are a big part of Wallin's business. "We look for children of all ages," she says. "In one project we needed twins that were three years old. That's a tough age. The younger they are, the harder to find." But Wallin comes through,

CREDITS INCLUDE:
The Emissary
Second Chances
Dillinger in Paradise
Madonna: The Early Years
Big Bad Beetleborgs
Mighty Morphin Power Rangers
Episodic

and producers call her when they're working on shows with young casts. "We have really extensive files," Wallin explains. "We also have a warm, friendly atmosphere, and kids feel comfortable coming here. Because they know we've done *Power Rangers* and *Sweet Valley High,* they automatically feel a sense of comfort, and not so much tension and fear. I think we're very patient"—and that's after seeing thousands and thousands of kids over a six-year period. Quite an accomplishment!

Despite the multitude of children who walk through the door at Katy & Company, it's not difficult to spot a winner. When casting *Second Chances,* for instance, Wallin probably saw 500 to 600 kids, and narrowed them down to three. "We ended up finding a little girl who had starred in *She's the Lovely,* with John Travolta and Sean Penn. Her name is Kelsey Mulrooney. She had this real soulful quality that just lit up the entire room. She did a scene that had the producer, director, and me in tears. Afterwards the director, a big man you'd never think would shed a tear, said, 'I need to take a break,' and got up and left the room, sobbing." The others chosen had also had prior acting experience. "They brought confidence and charisma into the room. Personality is everything. Confidence and charisma really come across during an audition, and you just light up when you see a kid with that attitude."

Of course, Katy & Company casts not only young people but adults as well. And, just as with the kids, it often takes days of poring over résumés to find the right look. A case in point is *Dillinger in Paradise*: "We probably saw more than 500 men between eighteen and thirty years of age for a very specific character. We looked and looked, but I just never felt we had the right actor. Four days before shooting, we had one last session, and a man walked in with this great personality, and when he started reading we knew he had it." Erin Beaux didn't have an extensive résumé, but he landed the lead. "That's what it's all about: finding actors to whom people respond so amazingly."

Training is a necessity. In Wallin's book, "classes are essential, because an actor must constantly grow and develop self-confidence. Through acting classes, you pour so much emotion into your work and target new issues, and you eventually blossom and gain more confidence."

Through confidence comes professionalism. "Coming into an audition professionally is so important. It's so frustrating when you give actors ample time to study their sides, and they come in with no concept. Every audition should be treated as if it were as important as a job, because it's what ultimately will get you that job," he says.

Wallin is always looking for readers for audition sessions, so a good way to make an impression on her is to be a good reader. She doesn't run lines with actors herself because she prefers focusing on them: "I can't give them my full attention when I'm reading. And I'm not an actress, so I'm concerned I'm not giving them a reading that brings them to a level I need to see. I stand apart from them and watch the performance. I feel it's a disservice to the actor if I read." She has a list of actors on whom she'll call to be readers. "It's the best opportunity for an actor to be able to participate in a casting session," she says. "You can truly see what goes on and the dynamics of the process. The more knowledge and information you can gain, the better the leverage you'll have in the industry." Wallin suggests sending a letter to casting directors, stating an interest in becoming a reader. You may get an audition out of it.

To Wallin, educating actors to the *business* of show business is one of the most fulfilling aspects of her job. "I do lots of lectures all over the country," she explains. "I talk about the obstacles they're going to encounter, how to overcome them, how to start looking at their job as work. I tell actors about developing a specific road map and tailoring it to themselves, because there really are specific things you need to know about marketing: head shots that represent you at your best, résumés with all the proper information, and so on. Many actors who come to L.A. wonder why they're so far behind. It's because they don't have the necessary information to compete in an industry where a lot of people do know the ropes."

She believes an actor must network in order to succeed. "Acquaint yourself with everyone in the business: casting directors, producers, writers, directors, and don't limit yourself to acting. Create and develop your own projects. Produce your own plays. The more active you are, and the more exposure you have, the more people you'll meet and the more you'll work. It's a business that's built on relationships—I cannot stress that enough."

Paul Weber

SLATER & ASSOCIATES

Associates: Mary Jo Slater, Jean Scoccimaro, Bruce Newberg
MGM
2425 Colorado Ave. #204
Santa Monica, CA 90404
(310) 449-3685

Acting was his passion when Paul Weber started out in regional theater. But it all changed when he moved to Los Angeles in the mid-1980s. "It was just at that point in my life when I thought being on the other side would be kind of interesting. The passion for acting seemed to disappear. It became more getting the job and making sure my insurance was covered, rather than the craft itself." So he decided to make the transition to casting.

"One reason I chose casting was that several experiences I had with casting directors weren't exactly actor-friendly." Weber wanted to change that and make the casting environment a place of comfort for struggling actors. "Having been there, I understood the mentality, the process, and the vulnerabilities of actors. My goal became to bring out the actor's best work."

His first casting job was as an assistant at Stephen J. Cannell Productions, where he worked on such shows as *Wiseguy* and *21 Jump Street.* He learned quickly what qualities worked best for actors at auditions. "Every actor who's interesting has something special that sets him or her apart from the others. It's that personal essence that makes it easier for me to see where an actor might fit in when I'm casting. It is so important for actors to know what is their essence as human beings," Weber explains. "Knowing your essence involves a sense of confidence, focus, and grounding that actors bring to a reading, as well as to their lives." And how does one attain these? "It's what you need to find within yourself," he says. "The only way is to experiment, to study, and even to travel and

CREDITS INCLUDE:
Tales From the Crypt
Reasonable Doubt
Poltergeist: The Legacy
The Outer Limits
Silent Cradle

meet as many people and allow yourself as many experiences as you can without judging. Then you'll have a foundation from which to build."

Actors who exude not only confidence but also a sense of humor make the best impression on Weber. "I love actors who are comfortable in their own skin, likable, and accessible."

He believes that actors also need to know their limitations. "Many actors feel they can play a lot of different roles, but you really have to know your range. It's important to be aware of how you are perceived, so that when you get to a certain point in your career, casting directors and others will be more inclined to give you some freedom of choice. You'll have more of an opportunity to tackle a different role once you've established yourself, not only in your craft but as an actor who can play within a range extremely well—and is now ready to push beyond it."

Training is vital to him (he himself attended the American Academy of Dramatic Arts). "I often read a résumé from the bottom up. I look for actors with stage training. TV credits may tell me you know how to make your way in the business, but are you comfortable in your craft as a stage actor? I may be biased, but I think not." Weber looks for an actor who makes interesting choices, and that actor is more likely to have come to him with formal training. "Newcomers will often underplay a scene at an audition. They think that doing less is more, but it's not, because they don't fill up the moments of a scene enough to make their choices interesting. Those with training, however, make a greater investment in their roles, based on the information they've gathered, and thus the scene is more interesting."

There are instances, he admits, when producers and directors will shy away from stage actors, fearing that their "larger than life" personas won't work on camera. "My advice," he suggests, "would be to think in terms of scale. The choices should be just as important, just as powerful, but the scale is different. If you're staging a sword fight, a large, slow thrust of the instrument would be appropriate. In film it might appear too big, and you might want to be closer to your victim and make the movement shorter and sharper. You're looking for the same result, the same motivation, but on a different scale."

Weber tells actors to be who they are, not try to be who they think the casting director is looking for. "You're either right for the role or you're not. Many times it's based on that inner essence I mentioned earlier. Sometimes the producer or director needs to feel that you can play the part when you walk in the door." Unless you're really good at it, if you try to put on a mask it won't work. "If, however, you aren't right for a certain part but do an interesting reading, I might not cast you for this project but I'll certainly keep you in mind for something more appropriate to your essence."

"I like someone who's done his homework," he says. "There are many who don't, you know. That only shows me they're not prepared or are hoping their good looks and credits will impress me." It's important to stay focused, he adds. "So many times between the audition and the callback the material gets over-rehearsed and the life is sucked out of it. I may give an actor an adjustment during the first audition. Take it, go home, get comfortable with it. Come back and do it. Just make sure you're really familiar with your dialogue and the choices you've made."

Weber encourages actors to continue to grow: "Being an actor is such a terrifying, unpredictable life, but it gives you such incredible opportunities. Whatever you do, whether it's in this business or not, everything you've learned can be used. Acting certainly has its perks: you never stop learning, and you never stop growing."

Ronnie Yeskel

RONNIE YESKEL CASTING

c/o Casting Society of America
606 N. Larchmont Blvd. #4B
Los Angeles, CA 90004
(213) 463-1925

There are two ways in which Ronnie Yeskel differs from the majority of casting directors: First, she hires readers to assist actors with their auditions; and second, she accepts phone calls. "I love actors," she declares. "I was an actor for about five minutes, so I know what a high you get when it's really working, and I know how hard it is to audition and try to land something in a several-minute audition." Yeskel agrees she's one of the most accessible casting people in the business. She also feels it's vital that actors have an environment that's comfortable to them.

Yeskel hires readers as a way of making actors feel more at home. Most are actor friends who wind up getting a role in the project at hand. The reader not only reads the scene with the actor who's auditioning, but also works with the actor, helping to make adjustments before the audition. The reader is used during callbacks for the producer and director. The only time Yeskel expects an actor to memorize a scene is when it's being taped, so that his or her face isn't buried in the script.

She requires actors at auditions to fill out a form that asks standard questions, including how to contact them or their agents (though to land a role with Yeskel it's not necessary to have an agent or be a union member). She'll also ask actors about prior experience and with whom they've studied. During the auditioning process, Yeskel encourages actors to ask questions. "This is their time to find out about the character. And if they're in the middle of a reading, and it's not going well, I also encourage them to stop and, if need be, to leave the room to

CREDITS INCLUDE:
Waking the Dead
Hope Floats
Permanent Midnight
Dr. Bean
Montana
Pulp Fiction
Reservoir Dogs

get into character." She realizes it may be their only shot, and she doesn't want them to throw it away needlessly.

In the way of dress, Yeskel prefers an actor to look the part as much as possible without donning a uniform or a G-string. What's more important is an actor's behavior. "I like an actor who's natural and funny. And I love actors who take risks, who don't know what they're going to do, who are not afraid to make asses of themselves." She believes that when an actor plays it safe, it's boring.

Casting against type is also important to this casting director; "it's more interesting, it's unpredictable, and you don't want to go for what's predictable." For *L.A. Law,* Yeskel tried to find unusual characters and would always seek a significant number of minorities to fill the bill. For *Waking the Dead,* starring Jodie Foster, Yeskel looked at actors from Los Angeles and New York to find the most interesting choices, and her casting "eye" was never more apparent than in *Pulp Fiction,* one of her most cherished accomplishments.

To Ronnie Yeskel "star quality" is more than just presence, it's eccentricity—maybe an offbeat look and, definitely, humor. "If you're funny, you can go very, very far. People love to laugh." It's obvious that Yeskel loves people, especially those in front of the camera, and she'll give her all to see that everyone gets a fair shot. "We go through every single picture that comes into this office. Hey, without actors, we're without jobs!"

PART TWO

The Casting Process

Musical Chairs

CASTING AND THE WORLD GOES 'ROUND

BY JOSEPH ABALDO

April 18, 1991

And the World Goes 'Round: The Songs of Kander and Ebb, currently at the Westside Theatre, was originally presented at the Whole Theatre in Montclair, New Jersey, as *And the World Goes 'Round* in June 1989. Casting director: Joseph Abaldo. Casting associate: Laura Richin.

August 25

Director Scott Ellis calls from L.A. to let me know that *And the World Goes 'Round* may get picked up for an Off-Broadway run. I told him it would be wonderful but encouraged him not to get too excited until it's definite. His enthusiasm, though, is infectious.

August 22

Scott Ellis called again from L.A., more excited. *And the World Goes 'Round* is looking very strong for an Off-Broadway opening this season. He reminded me not to get too excited but wanted me to be prepared in case it was to happen soon. Laura and I got my notes ready from the last call and alphabetized all the names of the actors already seen—those who were liked and called back, and those who were not—just in case.

September 7

Scott called from New York City this time. It's definite—we're a go. Peter Neufeld should be calling to make it official. The fact that Scott's in New York makes all this sound real, but there's nothing we can do till I'm officially hired. Laura suggests we prepare an idea list just for ourselves. We do—it's a good list!

September 12

Peter Neufeld and I begin negotiating. It looks like this is really going to happen. I ask for a meeting to discuss making offers to those in the original cast. Peter assures me that this is already being discussed. I start checking availabilities on the five actors.

September 17
Scott calls to bring me up to date on his casting ideas. In a meeting with Susan Stroman [the choreographer] and David Thompson [the co-author], the decision is made and approved by Kander and Ebb that the show would be stronger if we did some nontraditional casting and should encourage this idea in all breakdowns sent out. Fortunately, Laura and I anticipated this, and are able to read him a list of possibilities, both male and female.

September 24
Peter Neufeld and I decide that since one of our former actors is already unavailable and some of the others have other offers, we must consider all roles open till contracts are signed. Scott has been in touch with all the actors to keep them up to date and see if they are truly interested.

September 28
I meet with Karen Ziemba to discuss her moving to L.A. and why I feel she should postpone it, since she needs to be reviewed in New York. She's uncertain and has already accepted another job. Luckily she has a four-week out and we have some time. She's promised to keep thinking it over and keep me informed.

October 9
12:30: Susan Stroman calls to say that everyone in the show must move well. She reminds me that they all have to roller skate.
3:00: Susan calls again, this time to remind me that playing the banjo is essential for all five actors. She said we could teach them. She also stressed that we could teach them to roller skate, too.

October 26
Scott wants Laura and me to write the breakdown, keeping it as simple as possible, stressing the vocal. I remind him that the male understudy has to sing, dance (tap and jazz), roller skate, play the banjo, and also play the piano. I tell him this won't be easy. He says he trusts me; I laugh. I suggest a potential breakdown to read: "Seeking actors who can roller skate, dance, and play the banjo. Singing a plus." He laughs.

171

November 7
Laura handles the open call, which goes well. We find actors for our own file and have decided to bring some in to sing for Scott and Susan.

November 13-14
Each actor is told what we want them to sing, and the black actresses are asked to sight-read *And the World Goes 'Round*. All actors are told to bring their music in case Kander and Ebb want to hear additional material. The actors are excited to be singing for Kander and Ebb but also quite nervous. I tell them to relax—both Kander and Ebb are delightful.

November 16
The callbacks go very smoothly. The actors are extremely well-prepared. Every actress who sang *And the World Goes 'Round* sang it differently but very well. Toward the end of the day Adriane Lenox, an actress who was called back, asks to speak to me. She tells me to look around the Equity lounge. I do. Then she says, "If a bomb went off in this building, every diva in New York City would be dead." A few of the other actors hear her and say the casting of this would be tough. They all seem happy to be there.

Later, at the casting session, we knew we were making offers to Karen Mason, Jim Walton, and Karen Ziemba, all of whom had done the show for us last year. We narrow the ethnic female role to eight. Discussion begins; we cut to five. Discussion continues; we cut to three. Kander and Ebb decide they can cut no further and will leave the decision to Scott. I insist they give us their opinion and they do. The male role wasn't any easier; we were down to two and couldn't decide. Peter suggested we take the weekend to think it over—we agree. The understudy issue isn't easy, either. We postpone the male understudy decision but decide to offer the female understudy to Andrea Green.

November 20
After much discussion, the roles are offered to Brenda Pressley and Bob Cuccioli, and the male understudy to George Dvorsky. Everyone seems happy. Scott calls to thank us and say how excited he is. Within hours Peter calls to say that all conflicts—and there have been many—have been worked out and everyone has accepted. Laura and I are finished, and the work on the show can now begin.

Going First Class

WORKING ON *AIR FORCE ONE*

BY JANE JENKINS & JANET HIRSHENSON

Most people are aware that filmmaking is a long and difficult process, often taking nearly a year to complete. But few realize that just the casting process alone can take months.

Jane Jenkins & Janet Hirshenson, of the Casting Company, whose credits include *Jurassic Park, A Few Good Men,* and *Apollo 13* spent four months in 1996 with director Wolfgang Petersen casting *Air Force One.* In what follows, they share their diary of their work casting the Harrison Ford action-suspense film, one of the most popular releases of 1997. As it reveals Jenkins & Hirshenson's reliance on videotaped auditions in the casting of a major production, actors will note the importance of on-camera skills.

May 25, 1996
The producer, Gail Katz, calls to say she is sending over the script for the next film to be directed by Wolfgang Petersen. Upon receiving it, Janet decides to take a quick peek and then read it that night. But she can't put the script down. Exciting script!

May 30
Harrison Ford is already attached to the project; he'll play the President of the United States. We make initial casting lists for the characters of the First Lady, First Daughter, Vice President, and Korshunov, the villain.

June 30
We start looking at actors' demo tapes for the rest of the main roles. Having worked with Petersen and Katz previously, on *Shattered, In the Line of Fire,* and *Outbreak,* we've developed a system that works for them: looking at videotapes for the likely suspects. We continue

discussing the casting possibilities for the First Lady, the Vice President, and the villain. Next, we set aside dozens of tapes of those actors we liked for various roles.

July 11
The descriptions of the characters we need to cast go out from Breakdown Services to agents.

July 14
We start auditioning girls for the role of the First Daughter. We also accept submissions of videotapes from out-of-town girls.

August 8
Because we want real Russians to play a dozen or so roles, we start auditioning Russian actors. We continue looking at actors' demos.

August 11
We start auditioning actors on tape for the supporting roles.

Because we want people who actually have experience piloting airplanes for the roles of the pilots, we pull the pictures of actors who list *Pilot* on their résumé as a special skill.

August 20
We bring in the candidates for the roles of the First Lady and First Daughter to meet with Petersen, Katz, producer Jon Shestack, and Ford.

August 27
Petersen and Katz begin meeting the actors whose videotapes the director has liked. He has selected and meets only a few actors, those he has very strong interest in. We continue taping actors for the supporting roles.

September 1
Petersen and Katz start looking at the supporting players we have been taping. Decisions begin to be made, and we start making deals with the actors' representatives.

September 16
Principal photography begins on *Air Force One*. We continue taping actors for the roles still left open and a few that have been added during the production.

Where to Find Casting Directors

I f you live in Los Angeles or New York, it's not difficult to obtain a list of casting directors from one of several directories available at theater bookstores. They'll be glad to direct you to the annual and quarterly publications of organizations such as the Casting Society of America and Breakdown Services. But if you reside elsewhere, the number of casting directors are probably too few to warrant a guidebook. That doesn't mean there is no work in town, but perhaps that the several casting directors who are in business can handle the load. The question is: How does an actor find out who and where they are?

It may not be as easy as leafing through this book, but it's not an impossible task. First, you may know a local theatrical agent to whom you could turn. Reputable agents will know every casting director, since they work hand-in-hand. If you're unfamiliar with agencies, call a local theater and ask whom they rely on to cast their productions.

You could also check on-line if you have a computer connected to the Internet. Look up web sites in your city that are tapped into the actor's market. And possibly, you can get a free brochure from your state film commission, which often lists agents and casting directors. Perhaps you'll catch a news report that a film will be shot near you: Find out which studio is involved, call the production office at that studio, and ask who's casting the project. You may be referred to the person who's handling it locally. You have to be creative and put on your investigator's cap, but if you're determined, you'll succeed.

On the following pages are listed casting directors in United States and Canadian cities, beginning with Los Angeles and New York (for other California listings, see page 194). If you discover some that are not listed here, let us know so that we can include them in future editions. And good luck!

Los Angeles

Note: A number of casting directors are contacted through the Casting Society of America. They are marked with an asterisk (*). The address is as follows:

* Casting Society of America
606 N. Larchmont Blvd. #4B
Los Angeles, CA 90004
(213) 463-1925

Rachel Abroms
* c/o Casting Society of America

Cecily Adams
(see Liberman/Hirschfeld Casting)

John Aiello
* c/o Casting Society of America

Mercedes Alberti-Penney
224 E. Olive Ave. #205
Burbank, CA 91502
(818) 842-2270

Julie Alter
* c/o Casting Society of America

Deborah Aquila
Paramount Studios
5555 Melrose Ave.
Bob Hope Bldg. #206
Los Angeles, CA 90038
(213) 956-5444

Maureen Arata
* c/o Casting Society of America

Mary Gail Artz
Artz/Cohen Casting
5225 Wilshire Blvd. #624
Los Angeles, CA 90036
(213) 938-1043

Julie Ashton
Saban Entertainment
10960 Wilshire Blvd., 24th floor
Los Angeles, CA 90024

Simon Ayer
100 Universal City Plaza
Bungalow 78, first floor
Universal City, CA 91608
(818) 777-6748

Anthony Barnao
7333 Radford Ave.
North Hollywood, CA 91605
(818) 759-6942

Deborah Barylski
Walt Disney Studios
500 S. Buena Vista St.
New R-1, Room 5
Burbank, CA 91521
(818) 560-3570

Fran Bascom
Columbia Pictures
3400 Riverside Dr. #765
Burbank, CA 91505
(818) 972-8339

Pamela Basker
Warner Bros. Television
300 Television Plaza
Bldg.140, first floor
Burbank, CA 91505
(818) 954-4291

Lisa Beach
* c/o Casting Society of America

Ira Belgrade
5850-E West Third St.
Los Angeles, CA 90036
(213) 938-3800

Judy Belshe
(562) 434-0550

Annette Benson
Kushner/Locke Co.
11601 Wilshire Blvd., 21st floor
Los Angeles, CA 90025
(310) 445-1111

Chemin Bernard
Sunset-Gower Studios
1438 N. Gower St.
Bldg. 70, Room 211
Hollywood, CA 90028

Juel Bestrop
* c/o Casting Society of America

Sharon Bialy
3322 La Cienega Place
Los Angeles, CA 90016
(310) 558-5216

Tammy Billik
Walt Disney Studios
500 S. Buena Vista St., Bldg. R-1
Burbank, CA 91521
(818) 560-4087

David Bloch
(see April Webster)

Susan Bluestein
* c/o Casting Society of America

Eugene Blythe
Walt Disney/
Touchstone Television
500 S. Buena Vista St.
Team Disney Bldg. 417-K
Burbank, CA 91521
(818) 560-7625

Deedee Bradley
Warner Bros. Television
300 Television Plaza
Bldg. 140, first floor
Burbank, CA 91505
(818) 954-7841

Risa Bramon Garcia
* c/o Casting Society of America

Eve Brandstein
* c/o Casting Society of America

Megan Branman
Universal Television
100 Universal City Plaza
Bldg. 463 #112
Universal City, CA 91608
(818) 777-1744

Kate Brinegar
ABC
2040 Ave. of the Stars
Century City, CA 90067
(310) 557-6977

Jackie Briskey
* c/o Casting Society of America

Jaki Brown
(213) 856-6155

Ross Brown
Brown/West & Co.
7319 Beverly Blvd. #10
Los Angeles, CA 90036
(213) 938-2575

Mary Buck
Buck/Edelman Casting
4045 Radford Ave., Suite B
Studio City, CA 91604
(818) 506-7328

Perry Bullington
(see Bob MacDonald)

Jackie Burch
Ambassador Hotel
3400 Wilshire Blvd. Bungalow H
Los Angeles, CA 90010
(213) 252-6626

Victoria Burrows
11811 Olympic Blvd., Suite 105
Los Angeles, CA 90064
(310) 996-3127

Craig Campobasso
Pfillmco
11440 San Vicente Blvd. Suite 102
Los Angeles, CA 90049
(310) 571-9191

Reuben Cannon
5225 Wilshire Blvd. #526
Los Angeles, CA 90036
(213) 939-4190

Lucy Cavallo
CBS
7800 Beverly Blvd. #284
Los Angeles, CA 90036
(213) 852-2835

Lindsay Chag
Living Dreams Productions
11684 Ventura Blvd. #803
Studio City, CA 91604
(818) 769-9576

Denise Chamian
4113 Radford Ave.
Studio City, CA 91604
(818) 754-5404

Fern Champion
Champion/Paladini Casting
* c/o Casting Society of America

Brian Chavanne
Walt Disney/Touchstone Television
500 S. Buena Vista St.
Team Disney Bldg. 417-K
Burbank, CA 91521
(818) 560-7052

Ellen Chenoweth
* c/o Casting Society of America

Barbara Claman
BCI Casting
10834 Burbank Blvd.
N. Hollywood, CA 91601
(818) 755-9235

Lori Cobe-Ross
2005 Palo Verde Ave. #306
Long Beach, CA 90815
(562) 596-7406

Andrea Cohen
Warner Bros.
4000 Warner Blvd. Bldg. #27
Burbank, CA 91522
(818) 954-1621

Barbara Cohen
(see Mary Gail Artz)

Joanna Colbert
Universal
100 Universal City Plaza, Bldg. 488,
Suite 8A
Universal City, CA 91608

Cara Coslow
Carsey-Werner Studios
4024 Radford Ave., Bldg. 3
Studio City, CA 91604
(818) 760-6218

Allison Cowitt
(see Mike Fenton)

Dianne Crittenden
(310) 264-3913

Leah Daniels Butler
Warner Bros. Television
300 Television Plaza
Bldg. 140, Room 119
Burbank, CA 91505
(818) 954-7464

Anita Dann
270 N. Canon Dr. #1147
Beverly Hills, CA 90210
(310) 278-7765

Eric Dawson
Ulrich/Dawson/Kritzer Casting
3151 Cahuenga Blvd.West #310
Los Angeles, CA 90068
(213) 845-1100

Pam Dixon
P.O. Box 672
Beverly Hills, CA 90213
(310) 271-8064

Donna Dockstader
* c/o Casting Society of America

Christy Dooley
CBS Television City
7800 Beverly Blvd. #3371
Los Angeles, CA 90036
(213) 852-4501

Marion Dougherty
Warner Studios
4000 Warner Blvd.
Main Admin. Bldg. #117
Burbank, CA 91522
(818) 954-3021

Jonell Dunn
Walt Disney Studios
500 S. Buena Vista St.
New R-1, Room 5
Burbank, CA 91521
(818) 560-3570

Nan Dutton
20th Century Fox
10201 W. Pico Blvd., Trailer 703
Los Angeles, CA 90035
(310) 369-3387

Abra Edelman
Goodman/Edelman Casting
Mirisch Agency
10100 Santa Monica Blvd. #700
Los Angeles, CA 90067

Susan Edelman
(see Mary Buck)

Donna Ekholdt
20th Century Fox Television
10201 W. Pico Blvd., Trailer 730
Los Angeles, CA 90035
(310) 369-4501

Penny Ellers
(213) 876-1228

Rachelle Farberman
13601 Ventura Blvd. #686
Sherman Oaks, CA 91423
(818) 905-1806

Leslee Feldman
DreamWorks Casting
10 Universal City Plaza, 27th floor
Universal City, CA 91608
(818) 733-6411

Mike Fenton
Mike Fenton & Associates
14724 Ventura Blvd. #510
Sherman Oaks, CA 91403
(818) 501-0177

Mali Finn
MGM/United Artists
2500 Broadway, Suite E-5014
Santa Monica, CA 90404
(310) 586-8220

Jerold Franks
* c/o Casting Society of America

Carrie Frazier
HBO
2049 Century Park East, 36th floor
Los Angeles, CA 90067
(310) 201-9537

Dean Fronk
Pemrick/Fronk Casting
14724 Ventura Blvd. Penthouse Suite
Sherman Oaks, CA 91403
(818) 325-1289

Melinda Gartzman
Walt Disney Studios
500 S. Buena Vista St.
Old Animation Bldg. Room 2A
Burbank, CA 91521
(818) 560-7501

Scott Genkinger
(see Junie Lowry-Johnson)

Sara Getzkin
DreamWorks Casting
10 Universal City Plaza,
27th floor
Universal City, CA 91608
(818) 733-6820

David Giella
12711 Ventura Blvd. #170
Studio City, CA 91604
(818) 508-3361

Jan Glaser
Concorde–New Horizons Corp.
1600 San Vicente Blvd., 2nd floor
Los Angeles, CA 90049
(310) 820-6733

Laura Gleason
15030 Ventura Blvd. #747
Sherman Oaks, CA 91403
(818) 906-9767

Susan Glicksman
5433 Beethoven St.
Los Angeles, CA 90066
(310) 302-9149

Mary Goldberg
(310) 264-3939

Peter Golden
CBS
7800 Beverly Blvd. #284
Los Angeles, CA 90036
(213) 852-2335

Elisa Goodman
Goodman/Edelman Casting
Mirisch Agency
10100 Santa Monica Blvd. #700
Los Angeles, CA 90067
(310) 772-0722

Marsha Goodman
DIC Entertainment
303 N. Glenoaks Blvd., 4th floor
Burbank, CA 91502
(818) 955-5632

Lynda Gordon
(see Judy Taylor)

Jeff Greenberg
Paramount Studios
5555 Melrose Ave.
Marx Brothers Bldg. #102
Los Angeles, CA 90038
(213) 956-4886

Harriet Greenspan
NBC Productions
330 Bob Hope Dr., Trailer F
Burbank, CA 91523
(818) 526-2720

Iris Grossman
TNT
1888 Century Park East, 14th floor
Los Angeles, CA 90067
(310) 551-6352

Sheila Guthrie
(see Jeff Greenberg)

Sarah Halley Finn
Paramount Studios
5555 Melrose Ave.
Hope Bldg. #206
Los Angeles, CA 90038
(213) 956-5480

Ted Hann
Warner Bros. Television
300 Television Plaza
Bldg. 140, 1st floor
Burbank, CA 91505
(818) 954-7642

Bob Harbin
Fox Broadcasting Co.
10201 W. Pico Blvd.
Executive Bldg. 88 #325
Los Angeles, CA 90035
(310) 369-3847

Kim Hardin
Paramount Studios
5555 Melrose Ave., Trailer 10
Los Angeles, CA 90038
(213) 956-3319

Phaedra Harris
Cinetel Films
8255 Sunset Blvd.
Los Angeles, CA 90046
(213) 848-4385

Natlie Hart
Lapadura/Hart Casting
Edgar Scherick & Associates
1950 Sawtelle Blvd. #282
Los Angeles, CA 90025
(310) 575-5630

Geno Havens
Phoenician Films
8228 Sunset Blvd. #311
Los Angeles, CA 90046
(213) 848-3444

Karen Hendel
424 N. Lucerne Blvd.
Los Angeles, CA 90004

Cathy Henderson
Henderson/Zuckerman Casting
225 Santa Monica Blvd. #414
Santa Monica, CA 90401
(310) 656-3388

Marc Hirschfeld
Liberman/Hirschfeld Casting
4311 Wilshire Blvd. #606
Los Angeles, CA 90010
(213) 525-1381

Janet Hirshenson
The Casting Company
7461 Beverly Blvd., 5th floor
Los Angeles, CA 90036
(213) 938-0700

Alan Hochberg
4063 Radford Ave. #103
Studio City, CA 91604
(818) 505-6600

Judith Holstra
12725 Ventura Blvd. #1
Sherman Oaks, CA 91604
(818) 980-3022

Bob Huber
Fox Broadcasting Co.
10201 W. Pico Blvd.
Executive Bldg. 88 #324
Los Angeles, CA 90035
(310) 369-1820

Vicki Huff
* c/o Casting Society of America

Julie Hutchinson
20th Century Fox
10201 W. Pico Blvd., Bldg. 12 #201
Los Angeles, CA 90035
(310) 369-1892

Ruth-Ann Huvane
Columbia/Tristar
9336 W. Washington Blvd.
Culver City, CA 90232
(310) 202-3244

Elaine Huzzar
(see Johanna Ray)

Beth Hymson-Ayer
Hymson-Ayer Casting
Universal Studios
100 Universal City Plaza
Bungalow 78, first floor
Universal City, CA 91608
(818) 777-6748

Donna Isaacson
20th Century Fox
10201 W. Pico Blvd.
Bldg. 12 #201
Los Angeles, CA 90035
(310) 369-1824

Jane Jenkins
(see Janet Hirshenson)

Lorna Johnson
Warner Bros. Television
300 Television Plaza
Bldg. 140, first floor
Burbank, CA 91505
(818) 954-7644

Caro Jones Casting
Box 3329
Los Angeles, CA 90078
(213) 664-0460

Rosalie Joseph
MTM
12711 Ventura Blvd. #325
Studio City, CA 91604
(818) 508-3451

Holly Justo-Mosser
DreamWorks Casting
10 Universal City Plaza, 27th floor
Universal City, CA 91608
(818) 733-6683

Ellie Kanner
Raleigh Studios
5254 Melrose Ave., Suite 309-D
Los Angeles, CA 90038
(213) 960-3463

Christian Kaplan
20th Century Fox
10201 W. Pico Blvd.
Bldg. 12 #201
Los Angeles, CA 90035
(310) 369-1883

Nora Kariya
Walt Disney Studios
500 S. Buena Vista St.
Old Animation Bldg., Room 2A
Burbank, CA 91521
(818) 560-7501

Michael Katcher
CBS
7800 Beverly Blvd. #284
Los Angeles, CA 90036
(213) 852-2975

Beth Klein
Viacom
10880 Wilshire Blvd. Suite 1101
Los Angeles, CA 90024
(310) 234-5035

Nancy Klopper
* c/o Casting Society of America

Eileen Mack Knight
12009 Guerin St.
Studio City, CA 91604
(818) 752-1994

Joanne Koehler
Warner Bros. Television
300 Television Plaza
Bldg. 140, first floor
Burbank, CA 91505
(818) 954-7636

Allison Kohler
3322 La Cienega Place
Los Angeles, CA 90016
(310) 558-5216

Dorothy Koster
Crystal Sky Productions
9903 Santa Monica Blvd. #333
Beverly Hills, CA 90212
(310) 843-0223

Anna Marie Kostura
NBC Daytime Television
3000 W. Alameda Ave. #304
Burbank, CA 91523
(818) 840-4410

Carol Kritzer
(see Eric Dawson)

Jason La Padura
(see Natalie Hart)

Ruth Lambert
Walt Disney Feature Animation
500 S. Buena Vista St.
Burbank, CA 91521
(818) 560-9192

Geraldine Leder
Warner Bros. Television
300 Television Plaza, Bldg. 140, 1st floor
Burbank, CA 91505
(818) 954-7635

Keli Lee
Walt Disney/Touchstone Television
500 S. Buena Vista St.
Team Disney Room 417-C
Burbank, CA 91521
(818) 560-6566

Kathleen Letterie
Warner Bros. Television
3701 W. Oak St.
Bldg. 34R, Room 161
Burbank, CA 91505
(818) 977-6016

John Levey
Warner Bros. Television
300 Television Plaza
Bldg. 140 #138
Burbank, CA 91505
(818) 954-4080

Gail Levin
Hollywood Pictures
500 S. Buena Vista St.
Team Disney Bldg. #212D
Burbank, CA 91521
(818) 560-2085

Heidi Levitt
Television Center
1020 N. Cole Ave., 2nd floor
Los Angeles, CA 90038
(213) 467-7400

Meg Liberman
(see Marc Hirschfeld)

Tracy Lilienfeld
(818) 505-6615

Robin Lippin
NBC Productions
330 Bob Hope Dr., Trailer B
Burbank, CA 91523
(818) 840-7643

Marci Liroff
P.O. Box 48498
Los Angeles, CA 90048
(213) 876-3900

Leslie Litt
Warner Bros. Television
300 Television Plaza
Blvd. 140, first floor
Burbank, CA 91505
(818) 954-7073

Junie Lowry-Johnson
Paramount Studios
5555 Melrose Ave.
Von Sternberg Bldg. #104
Los Angeles, CA 90038
(213) 956-4856

Bob MacDonald
MacDonald/Bullington Casting
1645 N. Vine St., Penthouse
Hollywood, CA 90028
(213) 468-0599

Amanda Mackey Johnson
Mackey/Sandrich Casting
* c/o Casting Society of America

Mark Malis
Quantum Casting
3405 Cahuenga Blvd.
Los Angeles, CA 90068
(213) 874-4131

Debi Manwiller
Pagano/Manwiller Casting
20th Century Fox Studios
10201 W. Pico Blvd., Trailer 776
Los Angeles, CA 90035
(310) 369-3153

Irene Mariano
Warner Bros. Television
300 Television Plaza
Bldg. 140, first floor
Burbank, CA 91505
(818) 954-7643

Mindy Marin
Casting Artists Inc.
609 Broadway
Santa Monica, CA 90401
(310) 395-1882

Valorie Massalas
* c/o Casting Society of America

Eric Mathre
ABC
2040 Ave. of the Stars, 5th floor
Los Angeles, CA 90067
(310) 557-6547

Wendi Matthews
Fox Broadcasting Co.
10201 W. Pico Blvd.
Executive Bldg. 88 #320
Los Angeles, CA 90035
(310) 369-3849

Valerie McCaffrey
New Line Cinema
825 N. San Vicente Blvd., 3rd floor
W. Hollywood, CA 90069
(310) 967-6750

Kelly McDonald
Spelling Television Inc.
5700 Wilshire Blvd. # 575
Los Angeles, CA 90036
(213) 965-5789

Amy McIntyre Britt
(see Janet Hirshenson)

Jeff Meshel
NBC
3000 W. Alameda Ave. #231
Burbank, CA 91523
(818) 840-4729

Anna Camille Miller
Mystique Films Inc.
5400 McConnell Ave.
Los Angeles, CA 90066
(310) 448-7182

Barbara Miller
Warner Bros. Television
300 Television Plaza
Bldg. 140, first floor
Burbank, CA 91505
(818) 954-7645

Ken Miller
MTM
12711 Ventura Blvd. #325
Studio City, CA 91604
(818) 508-3341

Lisa Miller
Warner Bros.
4000 Warner Blvd., Trailer 43
Burbank, CA 91522
(818) 954-7586

Rick Millikan
20th Century Fox Studios
10201 W. Pico Blvd., Bldg. 75
Los Angeles, CA 90035
(310) 369-2772

Lisa Mionie
Raleigh Studios
5300 Melrose Ave.
Bronson Bldg. Room 203
Los Angeles, CA 90038
(213) 960-4931

Ed Mitchell
(see Robyn Ray)

Rick Montgomery
Montgomery/Parada Casting
1012 Fair Oaks Ave., Suite 218
S. Pasadena, CA 91030
(310) 841-5969

Bob Morones Casting
San Mar Studios
861 Seward St.
Hollywood, CA 90038
(213) 465-1874

Donna Morong
Walt Disney/Touchstone Pictures
500 S. Buena Vista St.
Casting Bldg. #10
Burbank, CA 91521
(818) 560-7875

Julie Mossberg
1875 Century Park East, 4th floor
Los Angeles, CA 90067
(310) 229-2479

Helen Mossler
Paramount Studios
5555 Melrose Ave.
Bludhorn Bldg. #128
Los Angeles, CA 90038
(213) 956-5578

Brian Myers
(see Marc Hirschfeld)

Nancy Nayor
Universal Pictures
100 Univeral City Plaza
Bldg. 507-3A
Universal City, CA 91608
(818) 777-3566

Bruce Newberg
Slater & Associates
MGM 2425 Colorado Ave.,
Suite 204
Santa Monica, CA 90404
(310) 449-3685

Sonia Nikore
NBC
3000 W. Alameda Ave. #231
Burbank, CA 91523
(818) 840-3835

Patricia Noland
NBC Productions
330 Bob Hope Dr., Trailer B
Burbank, CA 91523
(818) 840-7676

Lana Norlander
Warner Bros.
300 Television Plaza
Bldg. 140, Room 119
Burbank, CA 91505
(818) 954-7464

Pauline O'Con
ABC
2040 Ave. of the Stars, 5th floor
Los Angeles, CA 90067
(310) 557-6425

Michael O'Connel
(see Bob MacDonald)

Meryl O'Loughlin
7800 Beverly Blvd. #3305
Los Angeles, CA 90036
(213) 852-2803

Lori Openden
NBC
3000 W. Alameda Ave. #231
Burbank, CA 91523
(818) 840-3774

Fern Orenstein
CBS Entertainment
Design Center Bldg., Suite 311-D
Los Angeles, CA 90036
(213) 852-2862

Richard Pagano
(see Debi Manwiller)

Marvin Paige
P.O. Box 69964
W. Hollywood, CA 90069
(818) 760-3040

Mark Paladini
* c/o Casting Society of America

Dan Parada
(see Rick Montgomery)

Jennifer Part
United Paramount Network
11800 Wilshire Blvd.
Los Angeles, CA 90025
(310) 575-7019

Cami Patton
4063 Radford, Suite 106
Studio City, CA 91604
(818) 505-6608

Joey Paul
Nickelodeon
4040 Vineland Ave.
Studio City, CA 91604
(818) 753-3299

Donald Paul Pemrick
(see Dean Fronk)

Nancy Perkins
Universal
100 Universal City Plaza
Bldg. LRW, 9th floor
Universal City, CA 91608
(818) 777-2540

Julie Pernworth
NBC 3000 W. Alameda Ave.
Main Adm. Bldg. #231
Burbank, CA 91523
(818) 840-4142

Penny Perry
Lantana Center
P.O. Box 57677
Sherman Oaks, CA 91401
(310) 315-4868

Bonnie Pietila
20th Century Fox Studios
10201 W. Pico Blvd., Trailer 730
Los Angeles, CA 90035
(310) 369-3632

Christy Pokarney
Omega Pictures
8760 Shoreham Dr.
W. Hollywood, CA 90069
(310) 855-0516

Dana Polehanki
Paramount Studios
5555 Melrose Ave.
Hope Bldg. #206
Los Angeles, CA 90038
(213), CA 956-5480

Johanna Ray
Johanna Ray & Associates
1022 Palm Ave. #2
W. Hollywood 90069
(310) 652-2511

Robyn Ray
Mitchell & Ray Casting
626 Santa Monica Blvd. #302
Santa Monica 90401
(310) 275-1191

Robi Reed-Humes
Robi Reed & Associates
8170 Beverly Blvd. #202
Los Angeles, CA 90048
(213) 653-6005

Joe Reich
* c/o Casting Society of America

Barbara Remsen
Raleigh Studios
650 N. Bronson Ave. #124
Los Angeles, CA 90004
(213) 464-7968

Gretchen Rennell
* c/o Casting Society of America

Patricia Rose
Triangle Entertainment
9060 Santa Monica Blvd. #108
Los Angeles, CA 90069
(310) 385-0050

Stacey Rosen
ABC
2040 Ave. of the Stars
5th floor
Los Angeles, CA 90067
(310) 557-6789

Vicki Rosenberg
Sony Pictures
10202 W. Washington Blvd. #420
Culver City, CA 90232
(310) 244-5448

Donna Rosenstein
ABC
2040 Ave. of the Stars, 5th floor
Los Angeles, CA 90067
(310) 557-6532

Marci Ross
Walt Disney/Touchstone Pictures
500 S. Buena Vista St.
Casting Bldg. #10
Burbank, CA 91521
(818) 560-7510

David Rubin
8721 Sunset Blvd. #208
W. Hollywood, CA 90069
(310) 652-4441

Patrick Rush
(see Marc Hirschfeld)

Cathy Sandrich
(see Amanda Mackey)

Laura Schiff
2118 Wilshire Blvd. #338
Santa Monica, CA 90403
(310) 451-7320

Emily Schweber
(see Mali Finn)

Jean Scoccimaro
(see Mary Jo Slater)

Kevin Scott
Warner Bros. Television
300 Television Plaza
Bldg. 140, Room 149
Burbank, CA 91505
(818) 954-5138

Julie Selzer
Sunset-Gower Studios
1438 N. Gower St., Bldg. 5, Room 300
Los Angeles, CA 90028
(213) 468-3215

Tony Sepulveda
Warner Bros. Television
300 Television Plaza, Bldg. 140, 1st floor
Burbank, CA 91505
(818) 954-7639

Scott Seviour
The Disney Channel
3800 W. Alameda Ave.
Burbank, CA 91505
(818) 569-7542

Pamela Shae
Spelling Television Inc.
5700 Wilshire Blvd. #463
Los Angeles, CA 90036
(213) 965-5784

Mark Sikes
PM Entertainment Group
9450 Chivers Ave.
Sun Valley, CA 91352
(818)504-6332

Mary Jo Slater
Slater & Associates
MGM
2425 Colorado Ave. #204
Santa Monica, CA 90404
(310) 449-3685

Stanley Soble
Mark Taper Forum
601 W. Temple St.
Los Angeles, CA 90012
(213) 972-7374

Dawn Steinberg
Big Ticket TV
1438 N. Gower St., Bldg. 35, Box 45
Los Angeles, CA 90028
(213) 860-7425

Sally Stiner
Walt Disney Studios
500 S. Buena Vista St.
Animation Bldg. #2A
Burbank, CA 91521
(818) 560-2860

Randy Stone
20th Century Fox Television
10201 W. Pico Blvd.
Bldg. 54 #6
Los Angeles, CA 90035
(310) 369-4115

Ron Surma
(see Junie Lowry-Johnson)

Amy Taksen
Walt Disney/Touchstone Pictures
500 S. Buena Vista St.
Casting Bldg. #10
Burbank, CA 91521
(818) 560-7509

Judy Taylor
* c/o Casting Society of America

Mark Teschner
ABC Television Center
4151 Prospect Ave., Stage 54
Los Angeles, CA 90027
(213) 557-5542

Joy Todd
11811 W. Olympic Blvd. #105
Los Angeles, CA 90064
(310) 996-3127

Tina Treadwell
The Disney Channel
3800 W. Alameda Ave., 5th floor
Burbank, CA 91505
(818) 569-3281

Robert Ulrich
(see Eric Dawson)

Susan Vash
Paramount Studios
5555 Melrose Ave.
Von Sternberg Bldg., Room 101
Los Angeles, CA 90038
(213) 956-8377

Karen Vice
12001 Ventura Pl., Suite 203
Studio City, CA 91604
(818) 754-6548

Dava Waite
Universal Television
100 Universal City Plaza
Bldg. 463 #104
Universal City, CA 91608
(818) 777-1114

Katy Wallin
1918 W. Magnolia Blvd. #206
Burbank, CA 91506
(818) 563-4121

Amy Walpert
NBC Studios
3000 W. Alameda Ave.
Studio Bldg., Suite 2901C
Burbank, CA 91523
(818) 840-6593

Howard Warman
ABC
2040 Ave. of the Stars, 5th floor
Los Angeles, CA 90067
(310) 557-6932

Paul Weber
(see Mary Jo Slater)

April Webster
3960 Ince Blvd., Suite 115-117
Culver City, CA 90232
(310) 202-3534

Mary West
(see Ross Brown)

Ronnie Yeskel
* c/o Casting Society of America

Rhonda Young
ABC Pictures
2020 Ave. of the Stars, 5th floor
Los Angeles, CA 90067
(310) 557-7410

Dori Zuckerman
(see Cathy Henderson)

New York City

Amerifilm Casting
375 West Broadway, Suite 3R
New York, NY 10012
(212) 334-3382

Baby Wranglers Casting, Inc.
500 W. 43rd St., Suite 6G
New York, NY 10036
(212) 736-0060

Bass/Visgilio Casting
722 Broadway, Suite 6
New York, NY 10003
(212) 598-9032

Breanna Benjamin Casting
406 W. 31st St., 15th floor
New York, NY 10001
(212) 279-9876

Jay Binder Casting
513 W. 54th St.
New York, NY 10019
(212) 586-6777

Boricua Casting
153 W. 21st St., Suite 4
New York, NY 10011
(212) 627-1789

Jane Brinker Casting Ltd.
51 W. 16th St.
New York, NY 10011
(212) 924-3322
Submissions from agents only.

Kate Burton Casting
39 W. 19th St., 12th floor
New York, NY 10011
(212) 929-0948

CTP Casting
22 W. 27th St.
New York, NY 10001
(212) 696-1100

Kit Carter Casting
160 W. 95th St., Suite 1D
New York, NY 10025
(212) 864-3147

Donald Case Casting Inc.
386 Park Ave. So., Suite 809
New York, NY 10016
(212) 889-6555

Chantiles Vigneault Casting, Inc.
39 W. 19th St., 12th floor
New York, NY 10011

Aleta Chappelle
F. D. Productions
250 W. 57th St. #1516
New York, NY 10107
(212) 642-6355

Choo-Zee Casting, Inc.
315 E. 90th St., Suite 5W
New York, NY 10128
(212) 410-1647

Jodi Collins Casting
77 E. 12th St.
New York, NY 10003
(212) 982-1086

Comstock, Inc.
30 Irving Place, 11th floor
New York, NY 10003
(212) 353-8686, ext. 442

Contemporary Casting, Ltd.
Box 1844, FDR Station
New York, NY 10022
(212) 838-1818

Byron Crystal
41 Union Square West, Suite 316
New York, NY 10003

Sue Crystal Casting
251 W. 87th St., Suite 26
New York, NY 10024
(212) 877-0737

Merry L. Delmonte Casting
220 E. 42nd St., 28th floor
New York, NY 10017

Donna DeSeta Casting
525 Broadway, 3rd floor
New York, NY 10012
(212) 274-9696

Lou DiGiaimo & Associates, Ltd.
513 W. 54th St.
New York, NY 10019
(212) 713-1884

Joan D'Incecco Casting
630 Ninth Ave., Suite 3Q1
New York, NY 10036

Disney/Touchstone Television
500 Park Ave., 7th floor
New York, NY 10022
(212) 310-5596

Sylvia Fay
71 Park Ave.
New York, NY 10016
(212) 889-2626

Linda Ferrara Casting
217 E. 86th St., Suite 188
New York, NY 10028

Howard Feuer
c/o Casting Society of America
311 W. 43rd St. #700
New York, NY 10036
(212) 333-4552

Alan Filderman
(see Ortlip and Filderman Casting)

Leonard Finger
1501 Broadway #1511
New York, NY 10036
(212) 944-8611

Maureen Fremont Casting
150 E. 93rd St.
New York, NY 10128
(212) 289-7618

Doreen Frumkin Casting
18 W. 70th St.
New York, NY 10023

Godlove & Sindlinger Casting
151 W. 25th St., 11th floor
New York, NY 10001
(212) 627-7300

Wendy Gold Casting
39 W. 19th St., 12th floor
New York, NY 10001
(212) 795-3150

Maria Greco Casting
630 9th Ave., Suite 702
New York, NY 10036
(212) 247-2011

Amy Gossels Casting
1382 Third Ave.
New York, NY 10021
(212) 472-6981

Joey Guastella Casting
85-10 151st Ave., 5B
New York, NY 11414
(718) 835-6451

Carol Hanzel Casting
39 W. 19th St., 12th floor
New York, NY 10011
(212) 242-6113

Judy Henderson & Associates
330 W. 89th St.
New York, NY 10024
(212) 877-0225

Herman & Lipson Casting, Inc.
24 W. 25th St.
New York, NY 10010
(212) 807-7706

Billy Hopkins
Casting by Hopkins, Smith, Barden
19 Jay St.
New York, NY 10013
(212) 966-6000

Stuart Howard Associates, Ltd.
22 W. 27th St., 10th floor
New York, NY 10001
(212) 725-7770

Phyllis Huffman
1324 Ave. of the Americas
New York, NY 10019
(212) 636-5023

Hughes/Moss Casting, Ltd.
1600 Broadway, Suite 703
New York, NY 10019-7413
(212) 307-6690

Hyde-Hamlet Casting
Box 884, Times Square Station
New York, NY 10108-0218
(718) 783-9634

Impossible Casting
111 W. 17th St.
New York, NY 10011
(212) 924-7558
(212) 352-9098

Johnson-Liff Casting
1501 Broadway, Suite 1400
New York, NY 10036
(212) 391-2680

Avy Kaufman Casting
180 Varick St., 16th floor
New York, NY 10014
(212) 620-4256

KEE Casting
511 Avenue of the Americas
Box 384
New York, NY 10011
(212) 995-0794

Judy Keller Casting
140 W. 22nd St., 4th floor
New York, NY 10011
(212) 463-7676

Kipperman Casting, Inc.
141 5th Ave., 5th floor
New York, NY 10010
(212) 228-5551

Lynn Kressell Casting
445 Park Ave., 7th floor
New York, NY 10022
(212) 605-9122

Andrea Kurzman Casting Inc.
122 E. 37th St., 1st floor
New York, NY 10016
(212) 684-0710

Taylor Lewis
41 W. 56th St., 4th floor
New York, NY 10019
(212) 245-4635

Liz Lewis Casting Partners
3 W. 18th St., 6th floor
New York, NY 10011
(212) 645-1500

Vince Liebhart Casting
As the World Turns
524 W. 57th St., Suite 5330
New York, NY 10019
(212) 757-4350

Joan Lynn Casting
39 W. 19th St., 12th floor
New York, NY 10011
(212) 675-5595

John S. Lyons
c/o Casting Society of America
311 W. 43rd St., Suite 700
New York, NY 10036
(212) 333-4552

McCorkle Casting, Ltd.
264 W. 40th St., 9th floor
New York, NY 10018
(212) 840-0992

Abigail McGrath, Inc.
484 W. 43rd St., Suite 37-S
New York, NY 10036
(212) 564-7932

McHale Barone
30 Irving Place, 6th floor
New York, NY 10003

Philip Wm. McKinley
c/o Casting Society of America
311 W. 43rd St., Suite 700
New York, NY 10036
(212) 333-4552

Beth Melsky Casting
928 Broadway
New York, NY 10010
(212) 505-5000

Elissa Myers Casting
333 W. 52nd St., Suite 1008
New York, NY 10019

Navarro/Bertoni & Associates
101 W. 31st St., Room 1707
New York, NY 10001
(212) 736-9272

Nickelodeon
1515 Broadway, 38th floor
New York, NY 10036
(212) 258-7500

Orpheus Group, Inc.
1600 Broadway, Suite 611
New York, NY 10019

Ortlip and Filderman Casting
630 Ninth Ave., Suite 800
New York, NY 10036
(212) 459-9462

Joanne Pasciuto, Inc.
17-08 150th St.
Whitestone, NY 11357

Heidi Pellicano Casting
(203) 222-1957

Eileen Powers Casting
8 Fulton Drive
Brewster, NY 10509
(914) 279-5106

Scott Powers Productions
150 5th Ave., Suite 623
New York, NY 10011
(212) 242-4700

Michele A. Pulice Casting Partners
325 W. 37th St., 8F
New York, NY 10018
(212) 290-8240

Riccy Reed Casting
39 W. 19th St., 12th floor
New York, NY 10011
(212) 691-7366

Shirley Rich
Shirley Rich, Inc.
200 E. 66th St. #1202
New York, Ny 10021
(212) 688-9540

Richin Casting
33 Douglas St., Suite 1
Brooklyn, NY 11231
(718) 802-9628

Toni Roberts Casting, Ltd.
150 Fifth Ave., Suite 717
New York, NY 10011

Mike Roscoe Casting, Ltd.
153 E. 37th St., Suite 1B
New York, NY 10016
(212) 725-0014

Charles Rosen Casting, Inc.
140 W. 22nd St., 4th floor
New York, NY 10011

Judy Rosensteel Casting
43 W. 68th St.
New York, NY 10023

Selective Casting by Carol Nadell
Box 1538, Radio City Station
New York, NY 10101-1538

Caroline Sinclair Casting
NY Performance Works
85 West Broadway
New York, NY 10007
(212) 675-4094

Stage Door Enterprises, Inc.
400 Central Park West, Suite 3H
New York, NY 10025
(212) 865-3966

Elsie Stark Casting
39 W. 19th St., 12th floor
New York, NY 10011
(212) 366-1903

Adrienne Stern
149 Fifth Ave., No. 730
New York, NY 10010
(212) 253-1496

Irene Stockton Casting
261 Broadway, Suite 2B
New York, NY 10007
(212) 964-9445

Strickman-Ripps, Inc.
65 N. Moore St., Suite 3A
New York, NY 10013
(212) 966-3211

Helyn Taylor Casting
140 W. 58th St.
New York, NY 10019

Juliet Taylor Casting
41 W. 56th St., 4th floor
New York, NY 10019
(212) 245-4635

Bernard Telsey Casting
145 W. 28th St., Suite 12F
New York, NY 10001

Todd Thaler Casting
130 W. 57th St., Suite 10A
New York, NY 10019

Videoactive Talent
353 W. 48th St., 2nd floor
New York, NY 10036
(212) 541-8106

Joy Weber Casting
133 W. 19th St., 9th floor
New York, NY 10011
(212) 206-0001

Weist-Barron Casting
35 W. 45th St.
New York, NY 10036
(212) 840-7025

Grant Wilfley Casting
60 Madison Ave., Room 1027
New York, NY 10010
(212) 685-3537

Marji Camner Wollin & Associates
233 E. 69th St.
New York, NY 10021
(212) 472-2528

Liz Woodman Casting
11 Riverside Drive, 2JE
New York, NY 10023
(212) 787-3782

Other U.S. Cities (State by State)

ARIZONA
Darlene Wyatt
3625 N. 16th St. #100
Phoenix, AZ 85016
(602) 263-8650
FAX (602) 263-8890

ARKANSAS
Sarah Tackett
The Agency
910 W. 6th St.
Little Rock, AR 72201
(501) 374-6447
FAX (501) 374-8903

CALIFORNIA
(For Los Angeles, see p. 177)

Samuel Warren, Jr.
2244 Fourth Ave., Suite D
San Diego, CA 92101
(619) 264-4135
FAX (619) 531-1927

Judith Bouley
P.O. Box 22336
Carmel, CA 93922
(408) 646-9191
FAX (408) 646-1560

Barbara Shannon
1537 Rosecrans St., Suite G
San Diego, CA 92106
(619) 224-9555
FAX (619) 224-4261

Carissa Blix
Media Casting
6963 Douglas Blvd. #294
Granite Bay, CA 95746
(916) 652-3312
FAX (916) 652-8745

COLORADO
Colorado Casting Association
Peggy Larson
6795 East Tennessee Ave. #215
Denver, CO 80224
(303) 355-5888
FAX (303) 355-7839

CONNECTICUT
Judie Fixler Casting
Box 149
Green Farms, CT 06436-0149
(203) 254-7434

Lelas Talent Casting
Box 14
Milford, CT 06460
(212) 875-7955
(203) 877-8355

World Promotions
216 Crown St., 5th floor
New Haven, CT 06510
(203) 781-3427

FLORIDA

The Casting Crew
Cheryl A. Louden-Kubin
1948 Tyler St.
Hollywood, FL 33020
(954) 927-2329
FAX (954) 927-2371

Beverly McDermott
923 N. Golf Dr.
Hollywood, FL 33021
(305) 625-5111

The Casting Directors
Dee Miller
742 NE 125th St.
North Miami Beach, FL 33161
(305) 895-0339
FAX (305) 895-8608

Lori S. Wyman
16499 NE 19th Ave. #203
North Miami Beach, FL 33162
Phone (305) 354-3901
FAX (305) 354-3970

Unique Casting
Yonit Duchman
1613 Acton Rd.
Miami Beach, FL 33139
(305) 532-0226
FAX (305) 532-0996

Ellen Jacoby
420 Lincoln Rd. #210
Miami Beach, FL 33139
(305) 531-5300
FAX (305) 531-4748

Independent Castings
Kathryn Laughlin
8313 W. Hillsborough Ave., Bldg. 4
Tampa, FL 33615
(813) 884-8335
FAX (813) 884-9422

Lillian Gordon
13103 Forest Hills Dr.
Tampa, FL 33612
(813) 931-3252
FAX (813) 931-5030

Melvin Johnson
Universal Studios
1000 Universal Studio Plaza
Blvd. 22 #235
Orlando, FL 32819
(407) 363-8582
FAX (407) 224-6575

GEORGIA

Chez Casting
Shay Bentley Griffin
1776 Peachtree St. NW, #434-S
Atlanta, GA 30309
(404) 873-1215
FAX (404) 874-7532

IDAHO

Idaho Casting Company
Christine Wintergate
Route 1, Box J-56
McCall, ID 83638
(208) 634-8335

ILLINOIS

Jane Alderman
1633 N. Halsted
Chicago, IL 60614
(312) 397-0123
FAX (312) 397-0126

Brody, Tenner and Paskal
Jane Brody
20 W. Hubbard #2 East
Chicago, IL 60610
(312) 527-0665
FAX (312) 527-9085

Jane Heitz
920 N. Franklin #205
Chicago, IL 60610
(312) 664-0601
FAX (312) 664-3297

Beth Rabedeau
661 W. Lake
Chicago, IL 60661
(312) 207-6913

Dennis Hitchcock
P.O. Box 3784
Rock Island, IL 61201
(309) 786-2667
FAX (309) 786-4119

IOWA

Rodney Franz
503 W. Madison Ave.
Fairfield, IA 52556
(515) 472-8384

Susan Riedel
282 Kellys Bluff
Dubuque, IA 52001
(319) 556-4367
FAX (319) 588-3497

KANSAS

Joyce Cavarozzi
1544 Matlock Dr.
Wichita, KS 67208
(316) 683-4896

Linda Baska
P.O. Box 14061
Lenexa, KS 66285
(913) 631-0906

Stacey Mings/Vicki Evans
Wheeler Audio
4024 State Line
Kansas City, KS 66103
(913) 362-2500

KENTUCKY

Mina Davis
1120 Julia Ave.
Louisville, KY 40204
(502) 451-7923

K Casting
Merry Kay Poe
P.O. Box 22927
Louisville, KY 40222

LOUISIANA

Richard Castleman
202-30 Fifth Ave.
Covington, LA 70433

Dolly Dean Modeling and
   Career Network
Brenda Netzberger
3535 Sherwood Forest Blvd.
Baton Rouge, LA 70816
(504) 292-2424

Rick Landry
P.O. Box 51244
New Orleans, LA 70151
(504) 454-8000

Miriam Fontenot
119 Oren St.
Lafayette, LA 70506
(318) 235-6906

MARYLAND

Pat Moran
805 Park Ave.
Baltimore, MD 21201
(410) 244-0237
FAX (410) 385-2107

MASSACHUSETTS

Tighe and Doyle
Maura Tighe and Nancy Doyle
142 Berkeley St.
Boston, MA 02116
(617) 424-6805

Boston Casting
Angela Peri
1126 Boylston St. #211
Boston, MA 02215
(617) 437-6600

Collinge/Pickman
Carolyn Pickman
138 Mount Auburn St.
Cambridge, MA 02138
(617) 492-4212
FAX (617) 492-1306

MICHIGAN

The Talent Shop
Linda Lange
30100 Telegraph #116
Bingham Farms, MI 48025
(248) 644-4877
FAX (248) 644-0331

MISSOURI

Carrie Houk
6334 Alamo Ave.
St. Louis, MO 63105
(314) 862-1236
FAX (314) 862-1216

NEBRASKA
Actors, Etc.
Randy Nogg
9773 Lafayette Plaza
Omaha, NE 68114
(402) 391-3153

NEVADA
Marilee Lear
1112 S. Third St.
Las Vegas, NV 89104
(702) 459-2090
FAX (702) 459-3888

NEW JERSEY
Roz Clancy Casting
76 Wilfred Ave.
Titusville, NJ 08560

Paul Russell Casting
84 Essex St.
Hackensack, NJ 07601-4033

NEW MEXICO
Monica McDowell
P.O. Box 88
Chama, NM 87520
(505) 756-2389

NORTH CAROLINA
Fincannon and Associates
Mark, Craig, and Lisa Fincannon
1235 23rd St. North
Wilmington, NC 28405
(910) 251-1500
FAX (910) 251-9325

OHIO
Northside Films
Anita Daughtery
P.O. Box 6472
Cinncinatti, OH 45206
(513) 681-5767

OREGON
Megann Ratzow
8902 NE Milton St.
Portland, OR 97220
(503) 251-9050

Jed Shay
815 NW 13th Ave., 2nd floor, Suite C
Portland, OR 97209
(503) 227-2656

Jessica Stuart
4727 SW Vesta St.
Portland, OR 97219
(503) 246-4111

Nannette Troutman
1110 SW Salmon St.
Portland, OR 97205
(503) 241-4233
FAX (503) 241-4230

PENNSYLVANIA
Donna Belajac
109 Market St., 2nd floor
Pittsburgh, PA 15222
(412) 391-1005
FAX (412) 560-1005

TENNESSEE
Jo Doster
P.O. Box 120641
Nashville, TN 37212
(615) 385-3850
FAX (615) 297-6874

Tess Carrier
P.O. Box 11862
Memphis, TN 38111-0862
(901) 278-7454

Linda S. Dotson
123 Waltor Ferry Rd. 2nd floor
Hendersonville, TN 37075
(615) 824-1947
FAX (615) 264-0462

TEXAS
Shirley Abrams
P.O. Box 29199
Dallas, TX 75229
(972) 484-6774
FAX (972) 484-4995

Jo Edna Boldin
P.O. Box 151298
Austin, TX 78715
(512) 445-3203
FAX (512) 445-4208

Barbara Brinkley
1814 Briarcliff Blvd.
Austin, TX 78723
(512) 927-2299

Rody Kent
5422 Vickery
Dallas, TX 75206
(214) 827-3418
FAX (214) 827-2429

Liz Keigley
210 N. Hall Dr.
Sugar Land, TX 77478
(713) 242-7265
FAX (713) 242-8160

UTAH

Take One Casting
Cate Praggastis
5480 S. Woodcrest Dr.
Salt Lake City, UT 84117
(801) 355-2552
FAX (801) 272-3746

WASHINGTON

Kalles/Levine Casting
Patti Carns Kalles
506 Second Ave. #1525
Seattle, WA 98104
(206) 447-9318
FAX (206) 447-5669

Jodi Rothfield
2033 Sixth Ave. #306
Seattle, WA 98121
(206) 448-0927
FAX (206) 448-1016

Complete Casting
Stephen Salamunovich
2019 Third Ave. #205
Seattle, WA 98121
(206) 441-5058
FAX (206) 443-9814

Canadian Cities

Arnold Mungioli
Livent, Inc.
165 Avenue Rd.
Toronto M5R 3S4 Canada
(416) 324-5758
FAX (416) 324-5728

Lynne Carrow
P.O. Box 93011
W. Vancouver, BC
V7V 3G4 Canada
(604) 925-1092